The Ultimate Homeownership Guide

Tips and Tricks on How to Save and Make the Biggest Purchase of Your Life

Blue Peak Publishing

contained within this document, including, but not limited to, errors, omissions, or inaccuracies.

Table of Contents

Introduction

What's the point of saving money for a house? What's the point of saving money for anything, really? One thing that's never been in disrepute is the need to save money. It is basic and probably the most critical piece of financial advice you'll ever receive. We all know it's important to save, yet many people don't follow through on it.

But, when it comes to making sound financial decisions, the mere knowledge that you need to save is not enough. You should go a notch higher and understand why you are saving. This gives your actions a sense of purpose. It makes all your effort worthwhile. People say saving takes a lot of discipline, which is true. More importantly, saving takes a lot of sacrifices. So, the big issue for you should be whether the sacrifices you make toward saving money are worth it.

Now, let's talk about saving for a house.

Yes!

That's the answer to whether you think it is smart to buy a house.

Real estate is almost always a sound investment. The timing of the investment, however, is a personal choice, and this is where opinions might differ. For example, what's your motivation to buy a house? Is it because you are starting a family or because you've found a community that you think would be a perfect place for you to live? Are you buying the house, so you have a nice sanctuary when you retire?

We haven't even scratched the surface of reasons why you might want to buy a house. One thing that's certain, however, is that all of the reasons we've mentioned above are valid to each individual at a personal level.

Granted, most people wish to own a house at some point in their lives. The common stumbling block is the issue of affordability. Everyone has their dream house, one that completes the puzzle that is their lives. The challenge is getting from where they are today to owning that house. Houses don't come cheap either, which explains why it's important to start saving up for one—unless you are a celebrity and can buy a multi-million dollar home in cash.

So, assuming you have the money, what next? How do you go from having the money to finding and buying not just a house but the perfect house for you? That's what this book is about. Buying a house isn't like going to the mall and walking away with a house. You are not buying candy. A house is a huge and significant financial and legal undertaking. Yes, you read that right. There are legal aspects of buying a house that you take for granted at your own peril.

When we talk about buying the perfect house for you, this means a house that checks most of your boxes, if not all of them. The perfect house isn't just one whose market value you can afford, but one that you can also afford to maintain. It's about finding a house in a neighborhood that isn't too expensive for your financial status, or in a neighborhood where you aren't considered to be too wealthy, as you may become an unnecessary target for petty crime.

The perfect house is one that fits your budget. It's pointless buying your dream house if the utility costs bleed you dry every month.

The perfect house means one in a neighborhood that gives you easy access to all the social amenities your household needs. The last thing you want is your kids traveling a long distance to and from school every morning or spending long hours in traffic to get to your place of work. These are some of the considerations that go into buying a house that you'll learn about in this book.

Regarding the legal aspect of buying a house, unless you are buying the house in cash, you, like most people, will probably seek a mortgage or some other form of financial support to buy your house. These are legally binding contracts and breaching your contract will cause dire ramifications. Every day, people have their houses foreclosed; others must file for bankruptcy. Thus, if you are buying the house through some form of financing, you must scrutinize that contract and understand the consequences of failure to honor your end of the agreement.

Not to get you scared, though. This is just standard procedure for any contractual obligation. Always make sure you read the fine print and understand the kind of arrangement you are committing to.

There are perks to owning a house that you probably might not know about yet. For example, did you know you are allowed certain tax benefits by virtue of your ownership? When itemizing on your income taxes, you are allowed to deduct a portion or all your property taxes and mortgage interest. Those tax savings could go to any other project you are saving for. Apart from that, if you ever decide to sell the house, you can also enjoy significant reductions in your capital gains tax debt.

Taxes aside, owning a house will give you first-hand experience of the difference between renting. The rent vs. ownership debate is a discussion that has raged on endlessly for years on every platform. There are always valid reasons fronted by proponents of either argument. Indeed, it may be sensible and financially accurate to pay rent under certain circumstances, but the moment you own your house, everything changes. You start seeing things from a different perspective and enjoy the value addition that comes with owning a house. You can forget about those pesky monthly rent payments once and for all, right?

As you can see, saving for a house isn't just getting the right bank balance to take that house off the market. There's so much that goes into saving for and buying a house that you'll learn in this book to help you make the right choice.

So, back to where we started, why should you save money for a house? Well, ultimately, saving money gives you financial security. Saving money for a house and eventually buying that house gives you more than financial security. It gives you peace of mind. Owning a house is one of the surest ways of building your wealth and growing your portfolio. It is an accomplishment that many dream of, so pat yourself on the back for making the decision to achieve this feat.

Part 1:

Ready for Homeownership

Chapter 1:

Why Own a Home?

The argument for or against homeownership and renting has raged on for generations. Start it today in a group of your peers, and you'll continue that discussion for several days. This is proof that people still harbor different ideas on homeownership, all of which are valid. Owning a home is a big step, probably one of the most important decisions you'll make in your life. Therefore, it makes sense that you'd have to consider all your options and factor in all personal considerations before making this decision.

There was a time when owning a home would have been a no-brainer. While this may still apply to many people, it's not always a black and white decision. Besides, the economy has gradually evolved over the years, so there's a lot more to consider today than there were some years ago.

This book is about owning a home. For that reason, we'll shed more light on what it means and why it is important. Indeed, this doesn't take anything away from the value of renting a house. Eventually, these choices come down to personal considerations and making sure that your move is ideal for your circumstances.

Now, let's talk about owning a home. Why should you?

There's more to owning a home than just paying for it and moving in. Owning a home increases the value of your investment portfolio. Your house is an asset and, given the appraisals and appreciating values of homes over the years, it's safe to say that homeownership increases your overall net worth.

Buying a house is a long-term commitment. You are thinking about life decades from today. You are thinking about life long after you are gone, making sure your kids will have a place to call home, and so on. In fact, almost all decisions that go into finding and buying a house usually revolve around long-term considerations.

Finding the Right House

A quick online search today will reveal lots of houses in your preferred area. Some houses are marvelous works of art, while others need a lot of work. One of the first things to think about is your budget. An ideal house must be within your budget, or you might struggle to keep up with the mortgage payments and eventually lose the house. Before diving into budgeting, here are four important considerations that should guide you in finding the right house.

1. Your Financial Position

Before you start figuring out whether the house fits your budget or not, you must assess your financial situation. The house might fit your budget on paper but still overwhelm you in the long run. How much of your money is tied to servicing old debts? Can your income sustain you with an additional debt obligation? Do you have an emergency savings account to cushion you against unplanned expenses?

Owning a house is an exciting achievement. You must, however, be careful not to get carried away with the excitement and overlook the unexpected and unplanned financial commitments that come with it. Before you get excited about the house, do the math. If you are getting a mortgage, make sure you can afford the monthly payments.

2. Intention to Stay

Once you understand the long-term impact of buying a house, you need to look at the neighborhood or that city in general. Do you imagine yourself living there for many years? This isn't an easy decision to make. Think about it. If you have kids, they will eventually grow up and move away. How will that affect your residency in that neighborhood?

You should also think about your commute to work. Well, this is currently a gray area for many people, considering how COVID-19 has changed the work dynamics. Some companies have completely moved to remote working, regardless of the outcome of the pandemic. Others are transitioning to a hybrid working model, while others still look forward to having the complete workforce back in the office.

No one really knows what the future holds, so this decision will mostly be a speculative one. However, give it some thought, and make sure you are at peace with your decision thereafter.

3. Mortgage vs. Rent

There's a common misconception of comparing mortgage payments and rent payments. Some assume that if your payments are the same, you are ready to buy a house. Well, this might make sense on paper, but not in practice.

Granted, most people reading this book are planning to transition from rent to mortgages, and that's a good thing. Now, what you need to understand is that there are other costs in mortgages that you might not have factored into the rent comparison. Take taxes and mortgage insurance, for example. You probably didn't think about those, right?

For a first-time buyer, these might come as a surprise to you, and it gets worse that you can't really put an accurate estimate on them. Apart from the purchase-related costs, you must also think of the cost of maintaining that house. As a tenant, most maintenance costs like lawn care are often handled by the landlord. When you buy a home, this becomes your responsibility, among other additional costs that might be unique to that neighborhood.

Now, when you do the math once more, you realize that there's a huge difference between renting and buying with a mortgage. If you can comfortably manage all the extra expenses, then you are ready to buy a home. If not, you might need to go back to the drawing board and revise your checklist.

4. Household Needs

The cost of running a household goes beyond utility bills and lawn care. If you have kids, or you are planning to have kids, you should consider the financial impact of meeting their needs when choosing a house. They need to play, attend good schools, and so on. How will this affect your budget? Remember that children usually come with a lot of unplanned and unexpected expenses.

What if you have pets? Is the home you want to buy pet-friendly? Does it have a fenced-in yard? How much more will it cost you to make additional arrangements for your pets?

Benefits of Homeownership

One thing you can be sure of is that there will always be a house on the market that suits your needs. The challenge many people have is that they never take time to figure out what they are looking for in a house. As a result, they buy a house simply because it fits their budget, or it seems to have a lot of stuff that they like. That aside, owning a house is a good thing. Once you get beyond the misconceptions around homeownership, you'll realize how valuable a decision this will be, not just today but many years into the future.

1. Wealth Generation

Your house is a good investment, one that will play an important role in your pursuit of financial freedom. As much as there are good arguments for renting a house, many people realize later in life that they could have been able to buy a house much earlier with the money spent on renting. The last thing you want, as you grow older, is to have someone on your back every month demanding rent. That is money that could go towards your lifetime investment.

Financial experts often advise that homeownership is a sound savings plan for the long term. Indeed, you will still pay interest on the mortgage, but at the end of its term, you'll have a fully owned home. At some point, you may even decide to sell the house, usually at a higher price than what you purchased it for.

Homeownership also means building equity through the house, which essentially increases your net worth. Every mortgage payment is one less month until you completely own the house. It also means that the lender's claim on the house reduces as yours increases.

2. Tax Advantages

There are several tax deductions that homeowners enjoy. Whether you are single or married and filing separately, you'll always enjoy some tax deductions on allowable expenses. We will discuss this point in-depth in Chapter 8, including some of the deductions you can make to reduce your tax liability. Most of the tax benefits are useful during the early years of ownership because the amount you can deduct declines every year. This may also be the time when financial difficulties may arise as you start paying off the mortgage and reorganizing your finances. Tax deductions and anything else that could reduce your financial burden are welcome gifts.

3. Stability

More stability will come into your life once you own a house. At a personal level, owning a home is a huge achievement. There are many challenges you won't have to deal with anymore, for example, sharing your space with neighbors. If you are a private person, owning your space gives you more peace and stability.

Monthly mortgage payments also give you stability. Monthly mortgage payments are generally the same each month throughout the term of the mortgage. You know how much you owe each month and, if necessary, you can still negotiate with your lender for fairer terms depending on your financial situation.

If you compare this with renting, many landlords increase the rent each time the lease is renewed. Also, you are living at the mercy of your landlord. What if one day they decide they need you to move out because they want to use that house for some other reason? Of course, you'll receive a notice to vacate, probably in good time. You might even negotiate the notice and ask for more time as you figure out your next step. However, the fact is that you'll still need to move, which destabilizes everyone in your household. It doesn't matter whether you are moving to the next block or not. A move that you didn't intend or plan for is never a comfortable one.

4. Lifestyle and Personality

Imagine all the space you need, including a yard. You don't have to struggle to find parking for your second car. You don't need to worry about the noisy neighbors upstairs. Your kids have ample space and a yard where they can play, and you can also invite your friends and family over from time to time without worrying about any of the neighbors complaining. These are some of the benefits of owning a house.

When you are searching for a house in the market, you should look for features that will make you comfortable in that property before you commit and make a purchase. Prioritize what you desire and ignore the listings that do not meet your criteria. Ideally, when you settle on a house, you choose a house that will be suitable for everyone in your household. You choose a house that is perfect for your lifestyle and suits your personality.

Whether you are raising a family in your home or not, buying a house gives you the opportunity to create the kind of environment you love. It also comes with the accomplishment of seeing the transformation from a house to a home over the years. This can give your life an amazing lift, a feeling of wholesomeness and pride.

5.   Freedom to Modify the House

As a tenant, you know you can't just wake up one day and decide to paint the house a different color. You'd have to consult your landlord first, and there's no guarantee that they'll love the idea. A landlord will always put their interest first. For example, what if they allow you to paint the house, but soon after, you must move out due to unavoidable circumstances? The next tenant might not fancy your modifications, and the landlord will have to incur other costs to bring the house back to an acceptable standard.

These are the kind of problems you'll never have when you own your home. You can change whatever you want whenever you want to. If you decide to paint a new color every two years, no one will stop you (if the colors are approved by your homeowners' association). Need to replace some fixtures? Want to remodel the kitchen? Go ahead. Change everything you want. It's your house, after all.

6.   A Sense of Belonging

When you buy a house, you also buy into that community. You belong to something bigger than living in an apartment on a flat. In many communities, people look out for one another. This is good for security and your overall wellbeing.

You also have the pride of creating new relationships. By interacting with other homeowners, you get to learn so much about their experience in that community and what to expect, especially for your kids. This can be quite a revealing moment for you.

7.   Location Freedom

One of the main challenges of renting a house is that, in many cases, you are limited by your location. Some neighborhoods, as lovely as they might seem, might not have the kind of properties that you'd love to live in. You'd have to settle for whatever is available or simply move to a different location. In most cases, homely neighborhoods rarely have rental properties.

All this changes when you want to buy a house. Buying a house that works for you means that you've checked out several options in different neighborhoods and settled on one that checks most, if not all, of your boxes. You are free to choose wherever you wish to live.

The freedom of choosing where you want to live is one of the key advantages of buying a house. It's your money so let it work for you the way you want it to. Whether you want a house that's closer to your kids' school or closer to work, you'll always have more options with a home purchase than a rental property.

8. Boost Your Productivity

Thanks to the COVID-19 pandemic, there's been a seismic shift to remote working models. More people are working from home today than ever before. This work model might be here to stay, even beyond the pandemic. Many employers realized increased productivity from their workforce when people were allowed to work from the comfort of their homes.

Working from home takes away some of the challenges that would normally hurt your productivity in the workplace. For example, you work flexible hours. You can wake up at night and work or spend the morning with your kids and work in the afternoon. What's more important is that you meet your deliverables.

A good setup will improve your productivity. The fact that you also don't have to worry about what goes on at home when you are at work may ease your stress. Overall, working from home gives you a wholesome experience. While you can set up your workstation anywhere, even in a rental house, you are limited in the kind of modifications you can make to it. In your own house, however, you are free to design your home office however you want to. In fact, you might even get some tax deductions from it.

Chapter 2

How Much Home Can I Afford?

At this point, you understand the difference in value proposition between renting and owning a house and have probably made up your mind to buy a home! So, here's an interesting question: How much home can you afford?

This question is interesting because there's more to affording a home than paying the purchase price. If you are getting a mortgage, you really must rethink your approach to buying the house. This is a long-term plan, so your needs assessment comes down to things like your debt position and overall household expenditure against your total income.

Another crucial point to consider is the size of your home. You need a house that meets not just your needs but the needs of everyone in your household. Currently, most households need a home office, citing the shift to remote working models. Does the house you're considering have enough space? If not, can you conveniently create it without straining your budget? This is just one example of things you should consider before settling on a house you want to buy.

Now that you have all your non-monetary factors figured out and know how to make them work in the house you'll choose, let's talk about the money.

In terms of affordability, the simplest guideline to follow is the **rule of 36**. The **rule of 36** says that the total sum of your monthly debt payments should never exceed 36% of your gross income. Take a moment and list down all the debt payments you have. This includes the anticipated mortgage payments, property taxes, insurance, credit card debt, and student loans.

What we are doing here is making sure that your new house will not only fit your budget but will also give you room to live a normal, happy, and stress-free life. While the mortgage and allied payments might strain your finances a bit, you know that it's for a worthy cause. Therefore, the point is to make sure that your new home gives you as much financial security as it gives you peace of mind. You'll still need to shop for groceries, take the family out for those weekend hangouts, host your family when they come over, etc.

Why 36%?

Well, most lenders use this as the benchmark when determining whether you qualify for a loan or not. The idea is to make sure that you are not taking on a debt that will financially cripple you. We are talking about your debt-to-income ratio, meaning how much of your income goes towards paying off debt.

Some banks are flexible and can allow higher than 36%. However, if your debt-to-income ratio is higher than 43%, most banks won't approve your loan request. Those that do will charge higher interest rates to protect their interests, given that you are perceived to be too leveraged and a higher risk than most customers.

If your debt payments are 36% or less, you'll have more flexibility in your personal finances, meaning you have enough room to move your finances around in the event of an emergency and still meet your debt obligations. Let's assume a scenario where your debt-to-income ratio is 40%, which isn't overly high. You can still walk into many banks and get your mortgage approved. Now, the challenge here is that the slightest disruption in your household income or expenses could push you beyond the 43% mark. The moment your finances start to become strained, your chances of defaulting on your mortgage payments increases, resulting in the potential risk of losing your home.

Remember that this arrangement transcends your mortgage. It's also about honoring your obligations to the other debts you might be servicing such as your retirement plan, your investment budget, and your emergency fund. It's in your best interest to have your finances in order, including other financial obligations that might be of a personal nature. Buying your dream home should be an exciting and fulfilling experience.

Important Considerations

All lenders have minimum requirements you must meet to get your mortgage approved. These usually vary from one lender to the other and are mostly out of your control. Now, let's look at some factors you can control or influence, which will play an important role in determining how much house you can afford.

1. The Income Factor

Everything comes down to how much money you bring home every month. You might not be able to get a sizable raise, but here's one thing you can do—create multiple sources of income. If you've come this far with a single source of income, imagine how much pressure a second source takes off your income. With an additional source of income, you might be able to put a bigger down payment on the house, effectively reducing your monthly payments.

That aside, how secure is your current source of employment? You must be clear on this because anything that affects your income position might be a disaster for your homeownership plans. What happens if you lose your job? How soon can you get another? These possibilities give credence to the point we made earlier, creating multiple sources of income where possible.

2. Lifestyle Choices

What's your lifestyle? Are you living the lifestyle you desire? When it comes down to it, are you willing to change or downgrade your lifestyle to get your dream house? Lifestyle is mostly a matter of choice, and you should look at the bigger picture and take steps to reduce your discretionary spending. At times it's the simple things you need to move around to make it work. For example, you don't have to go to the mall every weekend. If you have several credit card accounts, you can figure out how to reduce or limit your exposure. When it comes to affording the house you want, you may have to take a more conservative approach to lifestyle choices.

3. Taxing your Budget

Did you know that some payments associated with your mortgage never go away, even after you are done paying the mortgage? Take property taxes, for example. It's important to know how much you owe so that you factor it into your budget. Local authorities determine property taxes, so it's good to find out the tax rates where you intend to buy a house. For planning purposes, the average nationwide rate is 1.1% of the assessed value of your home. This rate may vary from one place to another depending on the local tax regulations.

4. Insuring Your Home

Did you know that some lenders require proof of homeowners insurance before approving your home loan? It's in your best interest to get an appropriate homeowners insurance policy for your property. Each location is unique, so you must consider appropriate insurance coverage.

5. Maintenance Costs

Maintenance is one of the new expenses you'll be adding to your budget. Over time, your new home ages. And don't forget the natural effects of the weather. Apart from keeping your house looking mint and fresh, you also should think of the cost of maintaining appliances and equipment used in the house like the HVAC system, water heater, refrigerator, and oven. Think of the driveway, roof, sprinkler system, and patio. Other than keeping them looking new and fresh, it might also be good for your health.

6. **Utilities**

When you are shopping around for the perfect house, you must give some thought to the cost of running it, in terms of utility bills. Granted, you might be buying a house of the same size as the one you are currently renting, but the cost of utilities will never be the same. Look at the arrangement of the house, for example. How much natural light does it get compared to the one you are leaving behind? How are the rooms spaced? These are simple things that most people would ignore, but they eventually translate to how much you'll spend on heating and cooling the house as the weather changes.

Apart from that, you must also consider the normal cost of things like cable TV, garbage disposal, electricity, and water. The first few months of living in your new home may be a bit complicated for you and your family, considering that everyone is adjusting to living in a new house. Therefore, there might be an over-usage of utilities from members of your household, as they adjust to their new rooms and spaces.

If your commute has changed, you must factor this into your plans too. How much more fuel will you need every month? Will you have to use both cars, or is it time to sell one? Utilities are mostly unavoidable expenses; however, they ensure that you live a happy and comfortable life in your new home.

7. **Furnishing Your Home**

As you go from one listing to the other, think about how you will furnish the house and whether the present decor works for you. Your home should be a happy place for you, a sanctuary. This means that you'll want to arrange your house a certain way, possibly different from what you are used to in your rental. What else do you need to buy? Some windows may need coverings. You may need new furniture if you are moving to a bigger house. These are some of those costs that most people don't think about, but eventually, you must plan for them.

The House-Money Balance

What's the first thing that comes to mind when someone asks you, "How much house can you afford?" Most people will start thinking about their income. Others will mention what they think they want, or the kind of house they have been dreaming about. Each of these answers may be right or wrong, depending on the context of that question.

One thing that you need to understand is that the kind of house you believe you can afford with your current income isn't the same as the mortgage size that you can qualify for. Many people miss this point, and they often get disappointed when lenders are only willing to approve a smaller amount than what they had anticipated. Visit a few lenders and compare their offers before you start looking for a house. They'll want to know your financial profile to advise you on the kind of mortgage you qualify for and how to go about it. With this information, you can then start looking for a house, knowing at the back of your mind that lenders will come through for you.

Why should you do the extra work? Well, you might have a decent income that would qualify most people for a mortgage. However, you might not have a credit history, or your history might be insufficient. In most cases, the conversation with lenders is usually an eye-opener. You may realize that you have taken much for granted, or probably ignored some important things.

If you intend to take a mortgage on a house, it goes beyond your income. There are more costs involved in buying a house than the purchase price you see on listings. We will highlight most of the costs applicable in Chapter 5, giving you a clearer picture of the cost of homeownership.

In your conversation with different lenders, find out all the additional costs they usually charge borrowers, and from there, you can use a mortgage calculator to get an estimate of what it will cost to own a house.

More importantly, all the extra costs you will discuss are things that you cannot control. Once you sign the contract, you must pay them. One cost that you can control, which plays a big role in determining whether you can afford the house you want, is the cost of your lifestyle. Practically, when buying a new house, you may have to be a bit prudent about your finances. This means cutting back on vacations, eating out, partying, and so on. It might seem difficult at first but remember that you are doing all this for a worthy cause. The savings you make from cutting back on such lifestyle choices will go a long way in helping you afford the house you want.

Part 2:

How to Save Money for a House

Chapter 3:

Brilliant Ways to Raise the Money

At this point, you've completed your assessment and you understand what it takes to get that home you want. You know how much you need, the amount of house you can afford, how to work around your budget, and everything else that goes into financing your purchase. We now go a step further and figure out the most important thing, how to raise the funds you need. This is, after all, the end goal.

The estimated value of the house you want might seem to be an insurmountable task. How are you going to raise that kind of money? Well, many homeowners have been in this same spot before but, today, they are living happily and securely in their homes. How? It all comes down to planning.

With the right plans and mindset, you can set aside enough money for your down payment and even work harder toward paying off your mortgage earlier. What's interesting about the strategies we'll discuss in this chapter is that they are simple things we often take for granted but, if you do them consistently, the compounding effect over the years can make a big difference in your plans.

The next step in financing your home purchase is determining the amount of down payment required. How do you raise this money? Let's say you are putting a 10% or 20% down payment on the purchase price of the house, which is on the higher side, as many lenders will accept 3%. But, for planning purposes, let's work with the larger amount. After all, a larger down payment reduces the amount of your monthly mortgage payments. If you qualify for a VA or USDA loan, under certain circumstances, you may not need a down payment at all. We'll discuss these two loans later in the book.

Another reason why you may need to raise 20% of the down payment is due to the private mortgage insurance rule used by many lenders. Under this rule, you may have to pay for private mortgage insurance out-of-pocket if you can't raise 20% of the price. This is important to mortgage investors and lenders in case you default on the payments. Like we mentioned earlier, a 20% down payment isn't cast in stone. But it may save you a lot of money over the long term.

Let's look at some methods you can use to save money for your down payment.

Responsible Budgeting

If you ever need to save money for anything, the first thing you must do is be responsible with your budget. Budgeting helps you understand your household financial needs and manage your income better. As a matter of fact, it's almost impossible to divert money from your budget if you don't know how your money is spent. Responsible budgeting means you must be proactive with your money. Start by checking all your card payments and bank statements. This makes it easier to track your money.

What are you spending on most? What expenditure is unnecessary? What are the necessities? How much can you save by cutting down the unnecessary stuff every month? How much will you save at the end of the year? Now imagine how much you'd offset your down payment with that balance.

Resize Your Life

Now, the easier option is downsizing. But, for most people, this may mean taking drastic measures. You don't have to do that, hence resizing your life. You can save a lot of money by cutting back on your expenditures and living below your means for a while. You may even realize that your life is much better this way.

Rethink your loyalty to certain brands, for example. The most important thing here is to ensure that your needs are met. Review your necessities, or what you consider necessities. Are they true necessities? Start small, and then scale up the changes you make in your life. At some point, you may realize that it makes sense to downsize to a smaller house. If you have more than one vehicle, selling one might be a good idea. Eventually, you'll realize that the simple life isn't so bad after all.

Reinvent Yourself

One thing about saving to buy a house is that you are the only person who knows the kind of sacrifices you are making and why. Thus, don't lose sight of your goals. Reinventing yourself is about taking stock of your life up to this moment. What's your life about? What kind of lifestyle are you living? Are you happy with your life as it is? Do you need to stamp out some bad habits?

Before you started thinking about buying a house, for example, you'd spoil yourself impulsively. You may be the kind of person who falls into the "on sale" and "discount" traps frequently. Well, your priorities have changed now, so some of these habits need to be eliminated. Cancel unnecessary subscription services. Unsubscribe from email or SMS alert services that have fueled your impulse buying habits.

You love ordering in? Well, it may be time to try out your cooking skills more often. Meal deliveries are amazing, making your work easier most of the time. However, they are not kind to your pocket. Some of these decisions may not be popular with everyone around you. Explain to those who matter (your family) why you are taking these measures and get them to buy into your plans. This also makes it easier for them to adjust accordingly.

Get More Money

"Get more money" sounds easier said than done. The question is how do you do it? If you are at this point, it means you are probably not impressed by what's left of your salary after all your monthly bills and responsibilities are taken care of. This might be a good time to talk to your superiors about that raise.

Granted, this isn't one of the easiest conversations to have, but if you don't ask, you'll never know if it was possible in the first place. You must be strategic about this. Don't ask your manager about a raise when you are held up in the middle of a difficult project. The right time for this conversation is subjective, so you'll need to figure it out depending on the dynamics of your work relationship.

While it's good to be optimistic, there's also the possibility of your request being denied. What happens next? Well, you already have a plan to buy a house, so perhaps you need to start looking at other employment opportunities. If you can get a higher salary elsewhere, go for it. Note, however, that whatever your employment prospects are, you need something stable to buy a house. Don't get excited about the prospect of better pay on a short-term employment contract.

Alternatively, start that side hustle you've been putting off for so long.

Vacation? Not for Me!

You may have to forget about the vacations for a while. Putting a roof over your head takes precedence. Think about the last few vacations you've had. On average, most people spend thousands of dollars on a vacation, and that's just for one or two people. If your vacations include the kids, you are looking at upwards of $4,000 per vacation. That's money that could go towards your down payment.

Forget about the exotic vacations. If you must, you can have a good time in your city instead. You'll save on air travel, among other expenses. So, what can you do to have a good time now that vacations are out? Well, there may be quite a few historical sites and museums around. Certainly, you haven't checked them all out. What about a spa day at home? All you need is a personal kit, some YouTube tips, a few scented candles, and just like that, you have a spa day.

Debt Management

When you present yourself to a lender for a mortgage, they need to see you as a desirable borrower. Who is a desirable borrower? Someone who doesn't have a lot of debt. Note that lenders may also be skeptical if you don't have any debt at all. Most wouldn't want to be the guinea pigs in your debt journey. They want to see that you've owed someone else before, and you were responsible during the repayment process.

If you want to have good favor in the eyes of lenders, try and manage your debt before you submit your loan application. They'll compare your debt against your total income to see whether you are struggling to stay afloat or not. To get the best mortgage rates, try and reduce your debt before you submit your application. For example, you know that you want to buy a house in two years. Before you get there, embark on a thorough debt management drive and work around your debts so that by the time you apply for the mortgage, you'll be in a better debt position than you are today.

C'mon Guys, Help Me!

Asking for help never killed anyone, right? Asking for help simply means that you recognize the monumental task ahead and realize that you are surrounded by people who care and are willing to support your dream. Thus, there's no shame in asking for help. Those who are willing and able will come through for you.

Of course, you can't expect people to help you make the monthly mortgage payments—that one's on you. In the unlikely event that someone is willing to come through on this one, well, you can count your lucky stars. One area where people can come through for you in a big way is raising the down payment.

Apart from friends and family members, there are many people who have raised funds through crowdsourcing methods in the past. Realizing the financial challenges that people go through, many people have switched from bringing assorted gifts to weddings, birthdays, baby showers and other similar functions, to giving cash gifts. This makes a lot of sense. If you have an event coming up and people ask you the kinds of gifts you'd want them to bring, you can mention that you prefer cash and that you are planning to buy a house. Any contribution to your down payment would be highly appreciated. You'd be surprised at how many people would be thrilled with this idea and support you all the way.

When it comes to receiving such gifts, you must also be aware of the legal and tax implications. For example, if you are receiving gift money toward buying your primary residence, in most cases, there's no legal limit to the amount you can receive. However, if your down payment is for property other than your primary residence, for example, an investment property or a second home, then you are legally required to foot at least 5% of the down payment from your own pocket.

You must also understand the tax obligations of receiving gift money for your down payment. As the recipient, you won't assume any tax liability no matter how much money you receive. However, the person gifting you may incur gift tax if the amount gifted exceeds the annual limit allowable for exclusion. At the end of 2021, the annual limit was $15,000, according to the Internal Revenue Service (IRS). Thus, people can gift you up to $15,000 without reporting it for gift tax. However, if someone wishes to gift you more, they'd have to report it to the IRS and file a gift tax return.

Wow!! Who would have thought gifts were this complicated?

Save! Save! Save!

When it comes to raising money for your house, everything comes down to your personal effort. You can talk to your friends and family about gifting toward your home purchase, however, the bottom line is that your biggest effort will be concentrated around saving. You must learn how to save. All the options that involve other people may or may not work, especially since you cannot demand their help.

Let's say you are the type of person who struggles with impulse buying. You may know all too well that if you don't reel this habit in, you'll never make headway in your plan to buy a house. Well, one way of hedging this is to automate your savings.

There are now several options and products that can help you achieve this. First, you must figure out the amount of money you wish to save each month to achieve your down payment goal. Once you've done the math, contact your bank and inquire about making automatic withdrawals from your main account to a separate savings account created only for the down payment.

You are creating a standing order, so you don't have to worry about manually deducting your money from your checking account into your savings account. Such an automated savings system also helps you stay disciplined by making it difficult to access your money. This also helps take away the temptation of spending money on things you don't really need.

Finally, the point we have discussed above might seem subtle but, when done consistently, it can make a significant difference in taking you from point zero to owning a house. It all comes down to having a good plan and following it accordingly. A good plan starts from understanding exactly how much you need to raise then working your way up from there.

Part 3:

Funding Your House Purchase

Chapter 4:

The Reality Check—Credit Scores

At this point, you have a rough idea of what your ideal home will be: the purchase price, the down payment you are planning for, and you've probably identified the perfect neighborhood. It seems everything that goes into buying a house checks out. Well, not yet. One of the most important things in securing a mortgage, or any lending arrangement for that matter, is your credit scores. Credit scores can be the difference between manageable mortgage terms and an expensive mortgage. They might also determine whether you need a higher down payment on the house or not. We will discuss the dynamics of down payments in Chapter 10.

When planning to buy a house, credit scores are the ultimate reality check. Apart from determining whether you get favorable mortgage terms or not, your credit score may be the reason why you fail to qualify for a mortgage in the first place.

Even though credit scores can bestow some limits on your mortgage arrangements, you don't need to have a flawless rating to qualify for a mortgage. People have gotten mortgages with substandard credit scores before, so you shouldn't be overly concerned about having the highest rating. What you should focus on is the kind of opportunities that you can get with your rating and what you can do to improve and get even better terms.

In case you didn't know, credit scores simply measure your risk profile. They inform lenders of your ability to meet your expected loan obligations, in addition to your history with other creditors. Put yourself in the lender's shoes. Would you be willing to extend a $300,000 mortgage to a potential buyer if you can see from their credit report that they are constantly late on their car payment and struggling with credit card debt? This is an example of a high-risk borrower.

Some lenders may be willing to offer a mortgage to this type of borrower. However, since they already know the kind of risk they are taking, they may offset their exposure by charging higher interest rates than what they would charge low-risk borrowers. Apart from that, they may request a higher down payment on the house. This is a tricky situation because once lenders know that your history with handling debt is poor, it's not easy to renegotiate better terms with them. When you miss a monthly mortgage payment, the risk of defaulting on your loan is higher compared to someone with a stellar payment history.

Generally, good credit scores give you better opportunities and additional alternatives. A 620 credit score is enough to qualify for a mortgage for most loan programs. Any score higher than this further increases your bargaining power. If your score is 720 and higher, you can be sure you'll get the best or lowest interest rates on your mortgage.

Minimum Credit Score Requirements

Since the COVID-19 pandemic, many lenders have tightened the terms and conditions of their mortgages. This is in recognition of the fact that many people struggled financially in the wake of the pandemic and were unable to sustain their mortgage payments. To protect their interests, many lenders increased their minimum credit score requirements. You may have previously qualified for a loan with a lower credit score; however, these new developments could mean that you may need to make a larger down payment, contend with higher interest rates, or both. Consider working on ways of improving your credit score first before you apply for a mortgage. Let's have a look at the basic credit score terms on different mortgage arrangements below.

Conventional Mortgages

Conventional loans generally demand higher than average credit scores. You can still get lucky with a 620 credit score, but the terms may not be as favorable. On average, it's easier for your mortgage request to be approved with a credit score of 750 or higher.

The other benefit of having a high credit score is that lenders can do away with or significantly reduce the private mortgage insurance requirement. For example, with a 750 credit score, your mortgage insurance may be around 0.3% compared to 1.1% with a 620 credit score.

FHA Mortgages

If you don't fall into the category preferred by conventional mortgage lenders, you can try your luck with FHA mortgages. You may have your request approved with a 580 credit score. This also gives you a down payment allowance of 3.5%. If your credit score is lower than 580, you may only obtain approval with a 10% down payment.

While these are the basic approval conditions, lenders are at liberty to impose additional minimum requirements according to their business models. Therefore, if you only meet the minimum requirements, as per the FHA guidelines, you may have difficulty securing a mortgage approval with private lenders. While the FHA recommends a base score of around 580, private lenders can demand as high as 670 for FHA mortgages. Very few borrowers get mortgage approvals with credit scores below 600.

If a lender is willing to consider your application with a credit score below 600, they may demand additional information to get a better understanding of your financial position. For example, it's common for borrowers with credit scores under 550 to have their finances committed in liens, collection accounts, and judgments. For any lender to approve your mortgage in such a condition, they'd demand that you first clear most of these outstanding commitments.

VA Mortgage

The Department of Veterans Affairs doesn't have a minimum credit score requirement to buy a house. All they need is proof that you are either an active member of the military, a veteran, or a qualifying spouse of a veteran. With that in mind, private lenders who offer VA mortgages generally set their own credit score thresholds, usually between 600 and 650. Some may even go as high as 700.

USDA Mortgages

These mortgages, like VA mortgages, don't have a minimum credit score threshold outlined by the US Department of Agriculture. Lenders are therefore free to set their own thresholds. You should, however, have an easier approval if you score 650 and above.

Jumbo Mortgage

If your needs exceed the average conventional mortgage limits, you can apply for a jumbo mortgage. The terms here are stricter, and lenders will demand a credit score threshold of 700 and above. Given the high risk involved in such agreements, lenders generally prefer borrowers with a stellar credit score and solid financial health. For the best jumbo mortgage rates in the market, you'll need to score 740 or higher.

Determining Your Credit Score

How is your credit score determined? While it's important to understand your credit score and how it affects your ability to qualify for a mortgage, it's even more important to figure out the factors that determine your score. With this in mind, you can improve your credit scores to get better terms on your mortgage. Apart from improving your score, this information can also help you understand your risk exposure.

Though your credit score is key in determining the terms of your mortgage and whether you'll get approved, it's not the only thing that lenders look at. There are many other factors that help them establish whether you are creditworthy and can comfortably handle your future monthly mortgage payments. Because of this, the qualification benchmarks vary across lenders and the type of mortgage you seek.

Credit scores are obtained from an aggregate of reports from the three main credit bureaus (TransUnion, Experian, and Equifax). Each of these organizations has a unique credit scoring system. However, below are the main factors that cut across the divide, which influence your credit scores:

1. Payment History

This is perhaps one of the most important factors that determine your credit scores. Missed payments affect your credit scores negatively. Mortgage lenders like to see that you can pay all your debts on time. Payment history constitutes 35% of your credit score, so it's no wonder why you are often encouraged not to miss any payments on your debts. If you are missing payments, you may need to rethink your approach to managing your personal finances.

2. Credit Utilization

How much do you owe various creditors? This considers how you use different credit sources and is presented as your credit utilization ratio. Credit utilization is a function of your credit limits and your current level of revolving credit.

This ratio shows lenders how much of your available credit limit you are currently using. In essence, it shows how deep you are in debt. Having different sources of credit doesn't necessarily mean that you must exhaust your total available credit. If you use up most of your credit limits, lenders may believe that you are overly dependent on credit. Ideally, lenders prefer borrowers who use less than 30% of their available credit. Credit utilization makes up 30% of your credit score.

3. Credit History

The length of your credit history constitutes 15% of your credit score. Lenders want to know how long you've been managing various credit accounts. What's the oldest account on your credit report? How recent is your newest credit account? What's the average age of your credit accounts combined?

While it's easy to say that the longer your credit history is, the better, it's also important to highlight how you have been performing during that period. You can have a long credit history filled with missed payments, while someone else may have a relatively shorter credit history with stellar payment performance on all their credit accounts. The latter is likely to have a higher credit score. Thus, the context of your credit history matters more than the length of time.

4. Credit Mix

This is all about your credit portfolio. Lenders are also interested in the composition of your credit accounts. This gives them a summary of your credit burden. There are many sources of credit that may appear on your credit report, from student loans, to credit card loans, and car loans. This information also shows them how you prioritize your credit payments, so they can learn more about your credit management abilities. Some people pay off accounts faster by depositing more than the expected minimum payment. If you have such an arrangement in your credit mix, it shows the lender that you are a responsible borrower who goes out of their way to honor their debt obligations. This constitutes 10% of your credit score.

5. New Sources of Credit

Finally, lenders want to know about the most recent credit accounts you've opened. It shows them your immediate needs. For example, if you recently opened two or three new credit card lines, this could signal that you may not be a disciplined borrower. This information also constitutes 10% of your credit score.

Another important data point lenders look at is the number of hard inquiries from creditors on your credit report. Having too many hard inquiries on your credit report, within a short period of time, may indicate that you are having financial difficulties.

How to Improve Your Credit Score

Now that you know what makes up your credit scores, the next step is to figure out how to improve them. You understand that having a higher credit score may secure your mortgage approval, potentially without a substantial down payment.

All efforts to improve your credit score will center around the factors we described in the previous section. If you are having financial difficulties, you must identify the cause and how to fix it. Improving your credit will depend on your current credit profile and your commitment to strengthening it.

Obtain a copy of your updated credit report from any of the reporting agencies. Study the report and make sure that all the information contained in it is accurate. Identify the sections where you are performing poorly as those are the areas you must focus on. In the previous section we highlighted the percentage contribution of each of the main factors that influence your credit score. Spend more time on fixing those factors as a slight improvement could result in a considerable change in your overall credit score.

When it comes to improving your credit score, it's usually the simple things you may take for granted that count. For example, are your bills always paid on time? Imagine something as simple and routine like this contributes to 35% of your credit score. If you haven't been paying your bills on time, make that adjustment right away. List down all your bills and their payment due dates. Automate your payments or set reminders so that you never miss any again.

If you owe a significant amount of debt, try to pay the outstanding balances down. How quickly you can resolve this problem will mostly depend on the kind of debts you owe. For example, unless you win the lottery, you may be unable to clear student loans instantly. However, you can easily restructure your credit card debt to reduce your credit utilization ratio. This will improve your credit score faster.

Try to clear all your outstanding payments as soon as possible. Past due payments on your credit records are a bad idea. Late payments usually get reported in terms of the number of days they remain unpaid. The longer your outstanding payments remain neglected, the bigger the negative impact they'll have on your credit score.

Check your credit report for any erroneous information. You may have undesirable credit for mistakes that you did not make. This is also why it's always wise to check your credit report frequently. Dispute any inaccuracies with the credit reporting agencies as soon as possible so they can investigate it and make the necessary adjustments.

Finally, avoid making new requests for credit. Each time you request a credit account, the creditor performs a hard inquiry on your credit profile. Hard inquiries will remain on your credit report for up to two years. Multiple hard inquiries may alert a potential mortgage lender that you are likely experiencing a financial difficulty.

Do not default on any of your open credit accounts. Defaulting adds negative information to your credit report. Common examples include repossessions, charge-offs, and bankruptcy. The negative impact on your credit report can stay for years, with some lasting more than seven years.

Now that you know what to do about your credit report, is it possible to obtain a mortgage with bad credit?

Well, yes.

Even if your credit score is lower than the minimums we discussed for every mortgage type, you may still qualify for a loan. The challenge is that you'll have more hoops to jump through than the average borrower with better credit. That is because lenders may see you as a riskier borrower, hence the stringent requirements.

Lenders manage this risk with higher interest rates and larger down payments.

If you have no credit history, one option may be to have someone co-sign the mortgage for you. You'll have better luck if your co-signer has good credit. Additionally, you may ask one of your family members to buy the house on your behalf but add you to the title. This will give you the opportunity to work on improving your credit scores while living in the house. As soon as your credit profile significantly improves, your family member can refinance the house with your name included on the mortgage.

If none of these options are available for you, the best solution would be to put the idea of homeownership on hold and focus on improving your credit.

Chapter 5:

Closing Costs

The purchase price of the house is $300,000. So, that's all you need to move in, right? Well, no. This is the point where closing costs come in. There's a lot of mystery around closing costs, especially for first-time homebuyers. It's usually shocking to see the total price of a house. You may feel like you've been scammed. No, no one is scamming you. Closing costs are a real thing, and it's good to know about them so that you are not surprised when you buy a house.

Closing costs are processing fees that are paid to the lender, and they vary from state to state. These are the fees lenders charge for processing your mortgage. Think about all the professional work that went into making sure you that get the right house. For example, how did your lender verify the price of the house? They didn't just take the seller's word for it, right? They needed an appraiser to confirm whether the house is worth what the seller says it is.

You don't want a situation where you buy a house, and then a few years down the line, someone takes you to court for claiming ownership of their house, yet you've never paid them for it. It gets worse. That someone is a strange person you've never seen in your life. As it turns out, the person who sold you the house wasn't the owner. Well, your lender avoids such issues by making sure the title on that house is a clean title with no legal claim or pending legal issues by anyone else. That service isn't out of the goodness of their heart. It comes at a fee.

So, closing costs are mostly processing and convenience fees charged for different professional services that go into making sure you buy the right house. Apart from varying from one state to the other, closing costs will also depend on the type of mortgage you use to buy the house. For most mortgages, you will pay this fee in the meeting to close the deal on the house. This is the point where the lender receives your down payment on the house.

How much, on average, are you expected to pay?

These costs range between 3% and 6% of the market value of the house. If you took out a mortgage for a house worth $300,000, your closing costs would be between $9,000 and $18,000. Even though you can pay them both at the same time, your down payment is not apart of the closing costs.

Here's something many first-time buyers may not know. You may not have to pay closing costs. Most of these costs are negotiable. Therefore, you can negotiate with the seller to have them pay all your closing costs, or you can both share the costs. Clearly, that final lap of the home-buying process doesn't need to be a nightmare with unpleasant surprises.

Another interesting thing about closing costs is that they are not limited to buying a house. They also apply if you need to refinance a house, as they cover all the expenses necessary to finalize the transaction. Even though you can negotiate the closing costs with the seller, this isn't always guaranteed. Some sellers simply won't negotiate, and you'll have to pay all your closing costs. The seller has their own portion of closing costs.

It's good to know about these costs beforehand so that you can plan for them accordingly. Once you've settled on a house you like and figured out the amount of your down payment, it would be wise to talk to your lender about closing costs so that you know how much more you need to pay. The best way to handle closing costs is to pay them upfront as a one-time expense. Some lenders can include the closing costs into the mortgage, so you don't have to pay upfront. For example, if your original loan amount is $300,000, having 6% of this amount ($18,000.00) rolled into your loan would increase the amount financed to $318,000. The downside is that you'll be paying interest on those closing costs for the next 15-30 years.

To encourage first-time homeowners, some states offer grants and low-interest loans to cover closing costs. However, if you can raise the down payment, you can also raise the closing costs. There's no need to burden yourself with avoidable interest payments. Unless you are receiving a grant, try not to include your closing costs in the loan.

Before your settlement meeting, your lender should send you a Closing Disclosure document. This is where you'll find the relevant loan estimate for your house. If possible, go through it with an expert and ask all the questions you have. When you sit down with your lender to finalize the agreement, ask more questions, and negotiate anything and everything that you can. Remember, the most important thing is to walk away with not just a deal but the best deal.

Cost Liability

We've seen that you and the seller are both liable for closing costs. Now, let's say you find a good seller who's willing to negotiate some of the closing costs, also known as seller concessions. If you foresee difficulties obtaining the closing costs, let the seller know about it. They may just lend you a helping hand. After all, what's $18,000 compared to $300,000?

There may be a limit on how many concessions you can receive from the seller, depending on the down payment, occupancy, and type of mortgage. Generally, a larger down payment increases the seller's concession limits in conventional loans in any category. For example, if you are buying a primary residence, the seller can only support you up to 3% if your down payment is less than 10%, and up to 9% if you pay 25% or higher.

Seller concessions are usually based on the lower value between the purchase value of the house and the appraised value. There's no limit to the amount that sellers can contribute to other concessions like origination fees, credit reporting fees, appraisals, surveys, and discount points. Sellers may pay all the closing costs if the total is less than 3% of the value of the house.

Other than negotiating with the seller for concessions, you can also reduce the amount of your closing costs by comparing rates across lenders. Like the mortgage terms, take your time with closing costs too. Talk to different lenders, especially those that are actively competing against one another in the market. There's a good chance you'll get lower closing costs and competitive interest rates on the mortgage.

Also, it's easier for some sellers to agree to concessions because it guarantees them that their sale will be completed faster than if they hold out and let you handle the closing costs on your own. It's a win-win situation for everyone.

Let's have a look at the closing costs you can expect in your settlement. There are many costs involved, so we've grouped them into relevant categories for easier comprehension.

Loan Costs

From the title, you can tell these revolve around the loan you seek. They are as follows:

1. Application Fee

This should take care of everything that goes into processing the mortgage request, such as administration costs and credit history checks. The final cost depends on the steps needed to process your application, so it will vary across lenders.

2. Broker Fee

How did you obtain the mortgage? If you use a broker, expect them to charge a commission for their work. Broker fees are levied as a percentage of the loan amount of the home and range between 0.5% and 2.75%.

3. Underwriting Fee

The underwriting fee goes by many names, including the origination fee, processing fee, or administrative fee. This is what the lender charges to evaluate and prepare your loan. It includes costs such as the lender's attorney's charges, notary fees, and document preparation charges. On average, this fee is 0.5% of the mortgage amount you are borrowing.

4. Assumption Fee

This is only levied on assumable mortgages. An assumable mortgage is where you agree to buy a house from a seller, even though the seller is still servicing a mortgage on their house. In essence, you are buying out their loan with all the terms applicable on the remaining balance. The assumption fee isn't charged on the value of the house but on the outstanding balance of the seller's mortgage.

5. Attorney Fees

This fee isn't mandatory, however, in some states, real estate attorneys are legally required to be involved in closing the real estate transaction. Whether they are required in your state or not, it's always wise to have a real estate attorney involved to ensure you are buying a property without any pending legal liens. Be aware that most attorneys charge by the hour.

6. Prepaid Interest

Depending on the size of your loan, many lenders will insist that you pay the accrued interest on the mortgage before your first monthly payment is due. Thus, you may have to pay this at closing.

7. Discount Points

Discount points are fees paid directly to the lender in exchange for a reduced interest rate, thereby reducing the total amount of interest throughout the term of your mortgage. This is also known as an "interest rate buydown." One discount point is usually equivalent to 1% of the mortgage amount. Therefore, if you have a $300,000 mortgage, a discount point should be worth $3,000.

Mortgage Insurance Costs

Mortgage insurance is meant to protect your lender in case you default on the loan terms. It's not necessarily a mandatory requirement since you can waive it by depositing a minimum of 20% of the value of the house as a down payment. Here are some of the applicable charges:

1. Application Fee

Private Mortgage Insurance (PMI) is what we've previously talked about. It protects the lender, not your home. So don't think of it as insurance for your home and belongings. It is applicable if your down payment is less than 20% of the value of the house.

2. Upfront Mortgage Insurance

This is another cost that lenders levy to protect their interests in the contract. Your lender may ask for the insurance premiums on the first year's mortgage paid upfront. Another lender may ask you to pay a lump-sum amount covering the total premiums for the life of the contract. The terms of upfront mortgage insurance vary across lenders, but you can anticipate between 0.55% and 2.25% of the cost of the house.

3. Mortgage Fees

Mortgage fees and premiums depend on the type of mortgage you secure. Other than the insurance premiums, each of these organizations has different levies. For example, the USDA requires 1% of the mortgage amount upfront, 1.75% by the FHA, while the VA guarantee is between 1.25% and 3.3%. In each of these scenarios, the total upfront payment depends on the amount of down payment deposited.

Title Costs

Title costs go toward making sure that you are purchasing a house with a clean title. This means that no one has a claim on the house, for example, creditors or any other party who may dispute your legal ownership of the house. Here are some of the expected costs:

1. Title Search Fee

A title search determines the title status of the property. With proper documentation, it can be a fairly easy process. If not, it may drag on for a while and cost you more. This can happen when property records are not computerized. On average, title searches cost $200 but may vary depending on the company performing the title search or your state.

2. Title Insurance

Given the potential claims that can arise on a title, it's in the lender's best interest to ensure that their contract with you is safe. To this end, lenders' title insurance is an insurance policy protecting them in the event of an error or mistake on their end in the title search. This means that until your mortgage is completely paid, your lender is protected in case someone else claims that they have a right to the property after it's been sold to you.

If lenders can protect their interests, you can too. This is where you take owner's title insurance. It protects you against any claims or issues arising on the title after you close on the house. This coverage will last as long as you own the house, or in the event of your death, as long as your beneficiaries own the house.

The American Land Title Association levies between 0.5% and 1% of the price of the house for this policy. Title insurance can also be paid by the seller. In some cases, you might get a discount if both the lender and owner's policies are bought simultaneously.

Property Costs

These are costs in lieu of improvements done on the house and any other services that may be rendered to make sure you are getting the best value for your purchase.

1. Home Inspection

Home inspection fees are charged by most lenders, especially if your mortgage is backed by government programs. Lenders must ensure the house is fit for occupation, especially on structural grounds. Issues arising from the inspection can form a reasonable basis to negotiate a lower purchase price, or you can negotiate with the seller to have them fixed prior to the completion of the purchase. Alternatively, you can use the results of the inspection as a valid reason to cancel the contract altogether. This should cost you around $300-$500.

2. Appraisal Fee

You must have the house appraised. This is the only way the lender can justify the loan amount you are asking for. An appraisal also helps the lender determine whether they can recoup their money if you default on the loan. Professional appraisers charge roughly $400 for this service.

3. Annual Assessment Fees

This fee will depend on the neighborhood you are moving into. A local homeowners association may require an annual membership fee, which is usually paid upfront.

4. Property Taxes

At the point of closing, you may have to pay county and city property taxes for two months in advance.

5. Homeowners Insurance Premium

Before settlement, your lender may insist that you secure a homeowners insurance policy. This will safeguard your property against common risks like damage, vandalism, and theft.

These are the potential closing costs you may incur before buying the house. One important point to note is that all contracts and documents requiring your signature throughout this process are legally binding contracts. Take your time and go through them keenly. If you are unsure about anything, consult your attorney or an expert in the respective field. This will save you from many surprises. Also, remember that there's always room for negotiation with your lender, seller, or both. Negotiate your way into a better deal.

Chapter 6:

Lease to Buy Agreements

While the real estate market has often seemed a difficult venture for most people, one sure thing is that today we enjoy the luxury of opportunity. You don't need to have millions in your account to realize your homeownership dream. One of the many vehicles to ownership today is rent-to-own, also known as rent-to-buy or lease-option purchase.

This is an agreement where you, the tenant, live in a property and pay rent. After a specified time, you can exercise the option to buy the house. One good thing about this approach is that you get to try out the residence before committing to the purchase. Buying a house is a huge commitment, in most cases, a lifetime commitment. Many who buy a house right away don't get the benefit of trying it out. They must rely on research and whatever the real estate agent tells them about the property.

This is where the rental-purchase arrangement gives homeowners the advantage. Before you buy the house, you will have learned about the neighborhood, and more importantly, the costs of running the household.

Even though rental purchases are becoming more popular today, this concept has been around for a while. It's usually a two-part agreement, which includes the lease agreement and a purchase agreement to be exercised by the tenant if chosen.

The lease agreement is simply the same agreement you sign as a tenant stipulating the terms of your lease, amount of rent, and the terms or conditions of your tenancy in that property.

The purchase agreement stipulates the terms of converting your lease agreement into a purchase. This agreement can be exercised at the end of your lease agreement or while it's still in place.

The purchase agreement will also include details of the purchase, such as the agreed price of the property or how the price will be determined, and when. It also indicates whether your total rental payments will reduce the purchase price of the property or not and whether you need to deposit a down payment to exercise this option.

Let's explore this further in the next section.

The Finer Details

A portion of your rent should offset the purchase price of the house. Typically, the rental amount in these agreements is higher than a regular lease agreement. Once your lease expires, or at whichever time you determine with the owner, you can exercise your right to buy the property. Be mindful that the owner must acknowledge this in writing beforehand, especially the terms of offsetting the purchase price with your rental payments. When your option to purchase the house becomes available, you can proceed and buy the house through whichever means you prefer.

While this process is straightforward, the terms of such agreements may vary between states. However, it comes down to the agreement between the tenant/buyer and the property owner. Both parties must agree on all the terms, especially the purchase price, since the purchase will take place in the future, at a time when the owner may feel their house could be valued at a higher amount.

Given this consideration, some property-owners may price the property relatively higher than the current market value, so they can lock in the potential value gains. If the terms of your contract stipulate an appraisal before you buy the house, make sure that it also allows for you to hire your own appraiser. Often, the values determined by appraisers will differ. For that reason, the contract must also indicate how to address such outcomes.

Since you will have lived in the property for a while, there should also be an agreement on repairs and upgrades. Will the owner take care of these, or will you buy the house in its present state? How do these options affect the purchase price?

Finally, for a contract that involves depositing money into an escrow account, the best course of action would be to have your lender, bank, or a third party managing the escrow account, require both your signature and the property-owner's signature for access to this account.

Contract Types

There are two ways of going about this type of ownership. You can have a lease option or a lease purchase agreement. It's important to understand the terms of each of these alternatives, especially the kind of penalties that may apply in either scenario.

In a lease agreement, you pay the landlord a fee at the beginning of the lease as a guarantee that you will buy the house once your lease expires. In such an arrangement, your contract indicates whether part of your rental payments will offset the purchase price or not. You can negotiate the terms of this agreement, especially the amount you pay as rent.

You'll pay rent throughout the term of the lease; however, you can still negotiate the purchase price and terms with the property-owner. The lease option is perfect if you are not fully certain, at the beginning of the contract, that you'll buy the house. If, at the expiration of your lease, you decide not to buy the house, you can walk away from the contract, forfeiting your rent credits and the option fee paid to the owner at the beginning of the lease.

A lease purchase agreement is like a lease option agreement, but with a few modifications. First, your down payment on the house is funded by part of your rental payments. Remember that in the lease option, you can discuss and negotiate the purchase price with the property-owner during the lease, right? Well, in a lease purchase agreement, the purchase price is determined before you sign the agreement. This is also the time to set guidelines for an appraisal, such as the date and terms applicable.

Another important difference between these two contracts is that while you can walk away from a lease option contract and forfeit the option fee, this is not possible in a lease purchase agreement. In this scenario, you are legally bound to buy the house once your lease expires. With that in mind, make all the necessary arrangements to ensure you can buy the house at the end of the lease agreement. For example, determine whether your income and credit status can qualify you for a mortgage on that property. If you can't, you may have to concede your claim on the property once the lease expires, and you'll forfeit the rent credit earned during your tenancy. The property-owner may also reserve the right to sue for breach of contract if you don't buy the house.

Potential Risks

Lease-to-buy agreements seem like an amazing idea for both parties involved. The fact that you can lock in the price of the house before you commit to the purchase gives you a great opportunity to learn the neighborhood. On the other hand, the seller also has the benefit of a safe exit in that they can still walk away with some money if you decide to exit the deal. It looks like a win-win situation for everyone, right?

Well, there are some challenges you may experience as you navigate the housing market in this manner. Let's look at some of them to help you understand what lies ahead and decide whether the risks are worth taking.

1. **Expensive Arrangement**

The first thing you'll notice about lease-to-own contracts is that your rent payment will be higher than if you were in a regular lease. This is perhaps one of the biggest caveats with this ownership type. Most property-owners will increase your rent considering the contribution to your balance on the property. It wouldn't make sense for the owner to take the same amount of money from you as they would from someone else who was renting the property with no intention of purchasing it. This is also to protect themselves in case you decide to back out of the purchase agreement.

2. **Market Valuation**

Sellers have the highest potential for loss in this arrangement, and they are fully aware. Put yourself in the seller's shoes for a moment. If you knew you were engaged in a contract that may work, but if it doesn't, you may suffer a loss. What would you do? You'd probably find ways of hedging your potential loss in the contract, right? That's why most property-owners in such arrangements require higher rent amounts.

What does the seller have to lose?

In this arrangement, buyers have the advantage. The person who owns the house is at a disadvantage. If there's a boom in the housing market and property prices in the neighborhood appreciate, there's a good chance that you'll exercise your right to buy the house at the price you locked in at the beginning of the contract, which may be lower. The seller will have no choice but to sell, knowing that they could have sold the house at a fair market price. This also depends on the kind of value appraisal agreement you have with the owner.

A depressed housing market will see property prices falling, which would not make the purchase ideal for you. Therefore, you may decide to opt out of the deal. Alternatively, you may try to renegotiate the terms of your contract. Clearly, sellers are at a disadvantage in that they may end up holding onto a house whose value keeps dropping or sell a hot property cheaply. Given these realities, it's no wonder property-owners protect their interests by demanding considerably higher rent for such contracts.

3. Sharing Property-Owner Liabilities

Moving into a property-owner's house leaves you exposed to their financial challenges. For example, let's say the owner has a mortgage on the house and they have been having difficulties keeping current with the payments or even missed some payments. Their liability could be an inconvenience for you.

A lease to buy agreement means that you are tied to the seller throughout the term of your agreement. If, at some point, they are unable to pay any costs such as property taxes, the mortgage, or they have difficulties fulfilling any of their contractual obligations as the homeowner, parties to their contract may exercise the full extent of their rights to the property, thereby affecting your interest in the property. Your only recourse may be lengthy legal proceedings.

4. Non-Binding Sale Agreement

We mentioned earlier that sellers have the advantage in lease-to-own agreements. Fortunately, this isn't always the case. The fact that you have the option to buy the property doesn't mean that you have the right to buy it at any time after the contract expires. Your contract only gives you the option to purchase.

To protect their interests in the property, the seller may initiate a lease-purchase contract that requires you to buy the house. The challenge here is that lease-purchase contracts preempt the existence of good faith from both parties. You may be willing to buy the house, however, your finances may not allow it. If you are unable to obtain financing at that time, there's a risk that both parties to the contract will lose. As a rule of thumb, always read the fine print to understand the contract and clauses therein.

5. Potential for Loss

As the potential buyer, you have so much riding on this contract. You hope that events will unfold in your favor, allowing you to buy the house you love or to buy it at a lower price than the fair market value. In return, you agree to pay higher than average monthly rent. The additional sum is your investment in the property, which contributes to your down payment. We'll discuss the dynamics of down payments in Chapter 10, explaining how it becomes your investment in the property as equity.

Once the lease contract expires, you may have to speak to your mortgage lender about financing the purchase. At this point, the lender will evaluate your application and based on your credit score, and many other factors, decide the amount that they can accept as a down payment for the property.

The down payment value that your lender suggests may be higher or lower than the value you arrived at with your landlord. In this case, either the seller or the buyer will lose money when the house is sold. Remember that at the time you engaged the seller, you both agreed on an amount that would count toward your down payment. However, when the actual sale is taking place, your lender may not extend the same flexibility to you.

Protecting Yourself

Given the risks above, lease-to-buy agreements may still be a good way for you to get a better deal in the market, especially since you are only dealing with the seller. If this is the approach you choose, here are some useful tips to smooth over some of the risks:

1. Put Your Needs First

Don't be fooled by the goodness of the seller you are interacting with. This is a contract, and like every other contract, they are only willing to sell to you at the agreed price and under the agreed terms because it works for them. With that in mind, you also need to put your needs first.

Before signing anything, make sure you agree on contract terms that are ideal for you. Weigh the pros and cons of the options you are discussing and, if necessary, go over the contract with a professional.

It's better to take the extra precautions rather than signing a contract that won't work for you in the long run. If you are still unsure about buying the house, sign a lease-option contract. On the other hand, if you are certain this is the house you want, a lease-purchase agreement would be ideal.

2. Work with Professionals

The seller may not be interested in working with agents and other experts for their own reasons, but you should. A real estate agent, appraiser, and a real estate attorney will make a difference in your contract. Given their experience, they bring a different perspective to your contract, which can help you get the best deal.

Have an attorney review your contract before you sign. Although you may be on good terms with the landlord, there should be clear terms of engagement. For example, when is rent due? What's the arrangement if your rent is late? If you buy the house, which fixtures, appliances, or equipment are included in the purchase price? Who handles the repairs, maintenance, and homeowners association costs while your contract is still a lease?

3. Home Inspection

Before you commit to the agreement and sign a contract, have an inspector check the house. It doesn't matter whether the seller has their own inspector or not. It's in your best interest to have your own inspector. Some sellers may not be comfortable with this; however, you should still do it either way.

An inspector will let you know whether you are getting a good deal on the house or not. They'll also inform you about maintenance issues that you may have down the line. Many times, enthusiastic buyers rush into contracts without understanding major flaws that may pose a problem or become a regular cost later.

This isn't just about moving into the house. An inspector can also protect your interests by informing you of problems that you may have in the short term before your lease expires. Without their services, you may decide not to buy the house at the end of your lease agreement, only to receive claims for damages from the seller.

4. Lookout for Scams

People don't always act in good faith, even when it seems like the decent thing to do. Like every other contract that involves money, there will be unscrupulous sellers out there looking to exploit your inexperience. Some sellers may invite you to a contract when they have no intention of seeing it through to fruition.

How is that possible?

Well, this happens when they insert rigid clauses in the contract that allow them to easily cancel the agreement. When this happens, they retain all or a huge portion of the money you've paid so far, along with the rental credit. One common scenario where this happens is if you are late on a payment. Some sellers may exercise this right even if you delay payment by a few hours. If the calendar date has passed, they revoke your contract.

You should also be keen on the contract terms about repairs and maintenance. Customarily, such costs should be handled by the landlord. If that wasn't clear in your contract, the landlord could terminate your contract and claim that you neglected the property. This is one example where you may lose your money.

If you are about to enter into an agreement with a seller who doesn't own the property, then there's a good chance that you are being scammed. The target is the money you would normally pay up front.

Before you engage with someone in a contract, conduct a thorough search on the property. Find out if the person engaging with you as a seller has a legal claim on the property. More importantly, ensure that the property has a clean title, with no pending liens or issues. You should also check in the local tax records to ensure that you don't run into unnecessary problems with the IRS. Most of these checks can be conducted by professionals, hence the reason why you must never ignore their role.

Chapter 7:

Government Loans

There are many kinds of mortgage loans in the market, each designed with a different target audience in mind. This variety is due to borrower's unique needs that cannot be aptly met by a single mortgage program. For this chapter, we'll discuss some of the key mortgage options you may consider, which are offered by the government.

Note that these are not your only options. Depending on your immediate needs, you may also consider other mortgage options available through banks and other kinds of lenders in the market. Our discussion in this chapter will be centered around what your government can do for you to help you own a house.

As you try to obtain a good mortgage product that will meet your needs, you'll come across some terms that may be confusing if you don't know what they mean. Here are four of the most common, yet important, terms used to describe mortgages that you'll encounter:

- **Conforming mortgages.** These mortgages are offered within the local government limits.

- **Conventional mortgages.** These mortgages are not backed by any government agency.

- **Government-backed mortgages.** These mortgages are either issued or backed by the government or government agencies.

Now let's quickly have a look at the different kinds of mortgage products that are available in the market:

1.   Fixed-Rate Mortgages

From the name, you can tell that these are mortgages whose interest rates remain unchanged throughout the duration of the loan contract. These mortgages are the most popular among buyers, mainly because there are no surprise payment fluctuations after a few years into the loan agreement.

They are also ideal for borrowers looking for low monthly repayments spread over a long period of time. Many buyers opt for the 30-year fixed-rate mortgage because it allows them the flexibility of clearing their mortgage faster. This you can do by topping up your monthly repayments.

There is also the 15-year fixed-rate mortgage. Though the total interest paid throughout the term of the contract is less than longer-term mortgages, your monthly payment will be higher.

2.   Adjustable-Rate Mortgages

These are interesting products in that they encourage you to pay the loan faster. This kind of mortgage comes with two rates. The first rate is fixed, but for a limited amount of time. After that, the new rate kicks in, which is then adjusted every year.

The first interest rate is generally lower than most of the other mortgage rates available in the market, which also translates to lower monthly payments. Depending on the lender, the initial interest rate can be locked in for one year, five, seven, or even ten years.

This would be an ideal mortgage if you plan to pay off the mortgage while the initial interest rate is still in effect, or if you don't plan to have the mortgage for a long time. It would also be ideal if you believe that interest rates will be lower in the foreseeable future. If the initial rate expires, you may continue paying your mortgage at a lower interest rate.

3. Jumbo Mortgages

These products are designed for buyers whose needs cannot be met with normal conforming mortgage products. For example, if you are looking at financing a house that exceeds $647,200, which is the allowable maximum limit, in most counties, according to the Federal Housing Finance Agency (FHFA).

Jumbo loans are also known as non-conforming mortgages. They are riskier ventures for lenders because they are not protected if a borrower is unable to pay. They are available at either adjustable or fixed-interest rates but have stricter terms.

For example, you can only qualify for this product with a FICO score of 700 and above. Lenders will also insist that you have a considerable amount of cash in the bank — enough to cover at least a year of mortgage payments.

4. Interest-Only Mortgages

The monthly payments on these products are lower than most; however, they are not available for all borrowers. You must have good credit and sufficient assets to qualify for this mortgage. It is one of the most difficult products for the average homeowner to qualify for. If you qualify, you only pay the interest charged by the lender monthly. You don't pay back the principal.

They are mostly offered as adjustable-rate mortgages, with terms up to ten years. Once that period is over, your payments are amortized and split to cover the interest repayments and to reduce the principal amount. You could also refinance the mortgage or pay off the loan in full. Like the jumbo mortgages, you must show ample proof of your ability to pay the mortgage, which means you must have a considerable amount of valuable assets to support your case.

Government-Backed Mortgages

As we explained at the beginning of this chapter, these mortgages are either guaranteed or issued by federal agencies. There are many kinds of such mortgage products available; however, we'll only discuss the three most popular by application volume, hence the most important in this category, the FHA, VA, and USDA mortgages.

Federal Housing Administration (FHA) Mortgages

These mortgages are insured by the Federal Housing Administration (FHA). If you are worried that a low credit score or insufficient savings may be a stumbling block in your desire to own a home, this mortgage may be suitable for you.

The minimum requirement for an FHA mortgage is a credit score of 500. Some lenders will only accept credit scores between 580 and 620, citing the effects from the COVID-19 pandemic. With a higher credit score, you can access this product with a down payment of 3.5%. If you fall on the lower spectrum of the acceptable credit score, you will be required to produce a larger down payment, potentially 10% of the purchase price of the house.

Through the FHA's insurance, you can apply for this mortgage at a credit union, bank, or approved non-bank entities. Owing to this insurance, lenders are more willing to offer mortgages to borrowers who would not be able to qualify otherwise. After all, the government wouldn't default on its promise, right? Be mindful that this product can only be offered by lenders approved by the FHA.

With an FHA mortgage, you can buy or refinance your home. There are limits to the kind of homes for which you can obtain approvals. Covered under this program include single-family homes, multi-family homes with no more than four units, condominiums, and some manufactured homes.

First-time buyers prefer this product, given the ease of qualification compared to most of the conventional loans available in the market. The lower monthly payments to mortgage insurance are also an attractive feature, particularly for buyers with limited access to cash. You must be aware that FHA mortgages may include closing costs that aren't usually applicable in most conventional loans.

There are different types of mortgages available under this program, each whose limits vary from one county to the next. At the time of this publication, FHA loan limits are available in the range of $420,860 to $970,800. Other than the FHA's basic terms for qualification, individual lenders may have additional minimum requirements before you can be approved for a mortgage.

Veteran Affairs (VA) Mortgages

These mortgages are special products for active and veteran service members and their eligible spouses. If you've ever served in the military, this program is for you. Guaranteed by the US Department of Veterans Affairs, you can obtain a mortgage from approved private lenders such as mortgage companies, credit unions, and banks. The best thing about this mortgage is that if the appraised value of the house is lower than the sale amount, you won't need a down payment.

Terms on the VA mortgage are generally relaxed because of the government's guarantee to lenders, which also explains the flexibility on down payments. Not all lenders offer these mortgages. Therefore, take your time and look for lenders who doesn't just offer VA mortgages but does so at terms favorable to your situation.

Although the VA does not have a minimum credit score requirement for this product, lenders are free to set their own additional requirements. To this end, lenders will be interested in determining whether your income and debt position is sufficient to handle the monthly mortgage payments.

How much can you borrow under this program? As of 2020, borrow limits were abolished for active service members and veterans. If you are currently servicing or have defaulted on your VA loan, limits are still applicable. To this end, the applicable limit is in the range of $647,200 to $970,800, depending on your location.

You may still be able to get your mortgage approved for amounts higher than the limit in your county; however, a down payment is usually required.

So, how do you approach your application?

Well, first, you must get a certificate of eligibility from the VA. This is the proof your mortgage lender needs to establish your military credentials and that you meet the minimum VA requirements. You can get this certificate online or have it mailed to your address. Your lender can also request the certificate on your behalf. Next, find a lender who meets your needs, especially in terms of the kind of loan you seek and consideration of your credit. Finally, choose the home you want to buy, while making sure that it meets the basic requirements under this program.

US Department of Agriculture (USDA) Mortgages

This is a program designed for homeowners in rural areas who can prove economic need and are unable to secure the typical mortgage products. These loans are backed by the US Department of Agriculture and are issued through their Rural Development Guaranteed Housing Loan Program.

The goal of this program is to uplift and breathe life into rural communities by supercharging their economies. To this effect, USDA mortgages are offered at low-interest rates without down payments.

You can access this program in three ways, as a loan guarantee, a direct loan, or as home improvement loans and grants, depending on your immediate needs. One of the considerations to qualify for this mortgage is your income, whose limits depend on your location. Be aware that this mortgage can only be used to finance the purchase of a primary residence, of which you will be the occupant.

Another consideration is the total monthly payments to service the mortgage. All the payments due, including taxes, insurance, interest, and the principal on the mortgage must not exceed 29% of your income. Additionally, any other debt payment must not exceed 41% of your income, as this increases your debt-to-income ratio. The USDA may consider your mortgage application with a higher debt-to-income ratio if your credit score is higher than 680.

You must also have a clean credit history. To this effect, you may be disqualified if any of your accounts went to collections in the 12 months prior to your application unless you can prove that such action was warranted by factors beyond your control, for example, a medical emergency.

There are two possibilities, depending on your credit score. If your score is 640 and above, your mortgage processing should be faster and more straightforward. On the other hand, if your credit score is lower, you may have to jump through a few hoops to obtain approval. One good thing about this product is that you can obtain a mortgage even if you have a brief credit history, or if you don't have any credit history at all. In such a scenario, you may be qualified based on your payment history with utility bills and rent.

Other than the three mortgage plans we've discussed above, there are other government home loan programs that you may consider, depending on your plans. Let's have a look at some of them below.

1. Native American Direct Loans (NADL)

If you or your spouse is a Native American veteran, the government created the Native American Direct Loan program to help you finance your home needs. You can use this product to buy or build your house. You can also use it to finance home improvements or to refinance and reduce the interest rate on an existing mortgage on your home. Note that the home in question must be on Federal Trust land.

2. Rural Housing Repair Loans and Grants

This program runs under the USDA, offering loans and grants to homeowners with very low income in rural areas to help them improve, repair, modernize or remove health hazards from their homes. In most cases, those who apply for this loan are either on a restrictive budget or cannot access other forms of financing. The loan is repaid monthly at an interest rate of 1%, and the maximum loan limit is $20,000. This grant program is only available to residents who meet the requirements above and are age 62 years or older.

3. Section 184 Indian Home Loan Guarantee Program

This program runs under the Department of Housing and Urban Development (HUD). It is meant for families of Alaskan Native and American Indian origin, Native Hawaiians, Alaskan village tribes or households who are tribally designated under these categories.

If you fall into any of these categories, this program allows for relaxed credit terms and a lower down payment to fund your home purchase. You can also use this mortgage to finance new construction, improvements on your existing home, and to refinance your loan.

4. Home and Property Disaster Loans

If you are a homeowner or renting a property in a disaster area, this product is for you. Run by the U.S. Small Business Administration (SBA), this product gives you access to timely and affordable financial support if you live in an area classified as a disaster area.

These low-interest loans are long-term, up to 30 years, and are meant to help you rebuild your household from losses that may not be fully covered by some homeowners insurance carriers. You can apply for up to $200,000 to restore, repair, or replace your home to its condition before the disaster.

Note that you cannot use this product to make additions to or upgrade your home. Depending on the circumstances, you may also be able to use this product to refinance your mortgage if you don't have access to other loans but still need financial support to repair disaster damage that is not covered by insurance.

5. FHA Mortgages for Disaster Victims

Under the HUD, Section 203(h) gives the FHA the mandate to back mortgages for victims of a major disaster who need to either buy a new home or rebuild in the aftermath of a declared disaster. Your home must be in a disaster area or have sustained physical damage as a result of the disaster.

One thing you'll realize about each of the products we've discussed herein is that the terms will differ from one lender to another. Therefore, don't settle on the first lender you come across. Discuss your options with different lenders and, more importantly, question their flexibility on the terms of your agreement. Ensure that you choose an option that is suitable given your personal finances and your situation.

Chapter 8:

Tax Savings and Advantages

The reality of how much it costs to own a house can be daunting. As we said earlier, this is a long-term plan, so we soldier on and make it work. We'll discuss the tax breaks available to homeowners. It may not seem like much at the onset but when you add up the cumulative savings over the years, you'll have something to smile about.

Owning a home gives you the benefit of being able to live a comfortable life without the worry of monthly rent payments. It is also one way of creating a sense of stability in your life, especially when you have kids or if you are planning to have kids in the future.

Over the years, the government has worked to encourage more people to consider homeownership. This is in line with the need to give people a sense of belonging and stability. To this effect, the government, through the IRS, gives some concessions that come in handy for homeowners in terms of tax advantages.

Remember how hard you worked to raise the initial down payment on your house? Trying to save every possible dollar from your budget? Well, the same applies when it comes to tax advantages. There are several alternatives available that will work for you in one way or the other. In some cases, the tax deductions may not be significant, but it's still better than nothing, right?

To understand how tax deductions available to homeowners work, it's important that we first understand the concept of income tax deductions. Tax deductions reduce the amount of tax you owe to the IRS; however, this is only possible if you itemize the deductions.

Itemized deductions are allowable expenses you can subtract from your adjusted gross income (AGI), effectively reducing the amount of tax due to the IRS. Homeowners, and anyone who files income tax in general, have the option of either itemizing their tax deductions or claiming the full standard deduction according to their respective filing status.

By itemizing your returns, you have the benefit of choosing from any of the available individual tax deductions instead of taking a flat standard deduction. The question that many people ask is which is the better option. The correct answer is a matter of perspective. While itemizing deductions is preferred by many, it will only make sense if the cumulative value of your itemized deductions is more than what you'd get from the standard deduction. With that in mind, you must weigh your options carefully and choose that which gives you the best return.

You must also note that the amount of money you'll save from different tax benefits depends on your income and your filing status. For example, let's say a married couple and a single individual each buy a house where all the necessary features are similar, including the mortgage amount and deductions. Going by their filing status, the married couple will enjoy the largest amount of tax deductions compared to the single person. We must also emphasize the need to understand your tax liability to figure out whether itemizing is better than the standardized deduction. Generally, itemized deductions are ideal for homeowners earning a considerably high income, as well as single people.

Homeowner Tax Breaks

Owning and maintaining a household is generally quite a costly affair. You are responsible for things like repairs and maintenance on the property, in addition to other regular costs such as utility bills. Through the IRS, the government allows you some concessions to reduce some of these costs. Before we proceed, it's important to understand that tax breaks may vary from one state to the other, however, the breaks issued in many states across the country are similar to the federal tax breaks. Let's have a look at some of the deductions you can enjoy when you buy a house.

Mortgage Interest

We have discussed mortgage interest at length throughout this book, so, at this point, you should have a good understanding of what it is and why you may be required to pay it. The number of deductions allowable varies. You can usually deduct interest up to $750,000 of the mortgage debt you owe. If you are married and filing returns separately, each partner can deduct up to half of this amount ($375,000).

If you have a mortgage of $1 million or higher, you are limited in the amount you can deduct as mortgage interest.

Deducting mortgage interest isn't a blanket affair. There are some considerations that you must consider to qualify. For example, the mortgage interest deduction must be taken for your home, not anyone else's.

Any proceeds you receive as tax deductions can only be channeled toward improving either your primary residence or your second home. This includes buying the property, repairs, and any other cost that should add value to the home.

Going by these requirements, you can only claim mortgage interest tax deductions on your primary or secondary home. If you are using the property as an investment, this deduction will not apply.

Another important point you must note about mortgage interest is that it is levied as a depreciating factor. Thus, your mortgage interest is higher when you start servicing the loan and declines over the years. This also means that if you are enjoying any tax benefits from mortgage interest, your benefits will decline over the years. An exception to this rule is if your property taxes increase annually.

Discount Points

Are you paying discount points on your mortgage? We discussed the validity of discount points in Chapter 5 under closing costs and their impact on your mortgage arrangement. Discount points are allowable deductions, though the mechanism of enjoying the deduction may vary. By convention, discount points can only be deducted in the year you pay for the points, however, there are circumstances where you can deduct them throughout the mortgage term.

The IRS has tests to determine whether your discount points will qualify as a deduction or not. The purpose of these tests is to determine whether you are attempting to pass off mortgage fees as discount points when they are not. To this effect, you can only get tax breaks on legitimate discount points.

We also mentioned in Chapter 5 that, in some cases, the seller can pay the discount points. If this happened in your home purchase, you are allowed to include these points as a deduction when filing your tax returns. Be aware that you'll need to keep a copy of your tax return indefinitely in case you sell the house. When selling the house, you can use them to reduce the purchase price of the house by the amount the seller paid for the discount points.

Real Estate Taxes

State and local property tax deductions are limited to $10,000 a year and must be deducted in the year you paid for them. For married couples filing taxes separately, the limit is $5,000. The requirements for such deductions don't cut across the board. If you live in a state known for high income taxes and property taxes, you must confirm the state limits for deducting real estate taxes because you may not be allowed to deduct the entire amount.

Here's an interesting thing about real estate taxes. There are two kinds of tax liabilities, state sales taxes or state and local income taxes. The law allows you to deduct one, but never both. Therefore, your allowable $10,000 limit can only be implemented either on the aggregate of property taxes and state sales tax or property taxes and state and local income tax.

Home Office Deductions

Before the COVID-19 pandemic, not many people realized or took advantage of home office deductions. After all, most of the working population worked from company offices. Since the pandemic, remote working models have seen many people understand the importance of this deduction, but it also comes with some caveats.

By default, these deductions are only limited to individuals who use their homes exclusively as their primary business office. This includes self-employed individuals and small business owners. Going by this rule, employees who work from home cannot take this deduction.

The rules on home deductions are not black and white, hence the following exceptions:

1. If you store business samples or use part of your house to store inventory but your operation still doesn't meet the criteria for consideration as an exclusive business location, you can claim home office deductions.

2. If you have another structure on your property that you use for business purposes, even though it may not identify as the primary location for your business, you can also claim home office deductions.

Other than the exceptions above, you may also be able to claim home office deductions on mortgage insurance premiums, depreciation, utility costs, security systems, repairs, and maintenance.

Since more people are working from home because of the pandemic, there's a common misconception that almost everyone can now claim home office deductions. This isn't the case. If the government were to allow that, they would lose a lot of money. Besides, people set up their home offices in different ways, which could also make it cumbersome to come up with clear guidelines for all those who are working from home or those whose companies have embraced a hybrid working model. If the government wanted to offer concessions to people who are working from home, especially considering the pandemic, there would be other avenues that are more realistic and practical, such as income tax breaks.

So, to make things clear. Just because more people are working from home today doesn't necessarily mean that they qualify for home office deductions. If anything, only a handful will qualify, as per the guidelines we discussed earlier. According to the IRS, those who may easily qualify for home office deductions are independent contractors, self-employed individuals, and anyone who operates as a contractor in the gig economy.

Private Mortgage Insurance

Tax-deductible mortgage insurance, according to the IRS, includes the loan funding fee for VA mortgages, upfront mortgage insurance premiums on FHA mortgages, and the loan guarantee fee on USDA mortgages.

Note that this is only applicable to individuals whose income is not classified as too high. In this case, if your adjusted gross income is more than $109,000, you cannot qualify for this deduction. If you intend to claim this as tax deductible, you must be aware that your claim can expire. To be on the safe side, check to ensure that your claim hasn't expired for the present year.

Medically Necessary Home Improvements

If you must make any medical modifications to your home to make it habitable for your dependents or your spouse, you can claim these expenses as tax deductible. Some of the improvements that qualify under this category include railings, making your cabinets lower for easier access, installing lifts, ramps or expanding the doorways.

This deduction doesn't cover all enhancements, so you may make some valid improvements to your home but still fail to qualify for the deductions.

To qualify, you must first itemize the expenses you intend to claim. Apart from that, your claim cannot be more than 7.5% of your adjusted gross income. There's also the fact that some modifications may increase the value of your home. In this case, you can only claim deductions on the medical part of the expenditure going toward the improvements.

Capital Gains

The IRS is keen on taxing your profits. Thus, any time you sell something at a profit, they will be waiting for their cut. This is called capital gains tax and it is applicable if you decide to sell the house. The capital gains tax is waived if you have lived in the house for a total of two years during the past five years. Apart from that, under the capital gains tax exclusion, single people don't have to pay taxes on the first $250,000 of profit they make from selling their house, or $500,000 for married couples.

Once you buy a house, make sure to keep all the receipts and invoices for improvements and maintenance costs. You can add these expenses to the cost of the house, reducing the potential capital gains tax if you sell the house. This is probably one of the biggest tax breaks you can get from your house, so pay close attention to the repair and maintenance work that goes into your property.

Tax Credits and Deductions

These are important deductions because they reduce your tax liability for each dollar received in credits. For example, if you receive tax credits worth $2,000, you can deduct the same amount when filing taxes. On the other hand, tax deductions are applied as a function of your applicable marginal tax rate. Let's say you received a tax deduction worth $2,000, and your marginal tax rate is 22%. The $2,000 tax deduction would save you approximately $440.

For all the talk we've had about itemizing deductions, tax credits are only useful when you don't itemize them. On the other hand, tax deductions will be relevant if you itemize them. There are a few deductions whose adjustments will still be applicable without being itemized. These include contributions to your self-employed retirement fund, IRA contributions, interest on student loans, and any moving expenses applicable if you are a member of the armed forces.

Energy Efficiency

The government also allows you to deduct tax credits for making your home energy efficient. Some of the expenses that may count include adding fuel cells, using small wind turbines, geothermal heat pumps, or any form of solar power equipment.

Tax deductions are an interesting concept. As soon as you start identifying the potential tax savings in your home, you may get carried away and contemplate adding other home expenses to increase your total tax deductions. The IRS is aware that homeowners may attempt to do this. For that reason, below are some of the expenses in your home that are not deductible:

- depreciation

- down payment on your home

- fire insurance

- domestic service costs

- mortgage principal amount

- homeowners insurance premiums

- utility bills

Finally, as tempting as it may seem, you can't deduct all your household expenses for tax purposes. If you are ever in doubt or unsure about anything, speak with a CPA or tax professional for clarification. As you can imagine, it may take you countless hours to figure out these tax breaks. You can save a lot of time and money by having the experts handle this for you. A professional can potentially find tax credits and deductions that you may not be aware of. Besides, preparing taxes can be complicated, so it's better to get an expert involved and watch your money work for you.

Part 4:

Let's Get Your Home!

Chapter 9:

What to Look for When Buying a House

At this point, you've figured out everything you need to know about homeownership. All that's left to do is identify a house and sign the contract. In this chapter, we'll discuss important points you must consider for finding the right house.

The factors we'll discuss in this section are vital for two reasons. One, you need to buy a home that suits your needs. Two, when you buy a home, you need to make sure that the running costs won't kill you. Somehow, people ignore that second point. Can you afford the heating and lighting requirements of that home? How about access to the things you are used to? Does your commute to work or school for your kids become cheaper or more expensive? If you don't consider these factors, your dream home may soon become a nightmare for your bank account and your household in general.

The Role of Real Estate Agents

Hate them or love them, real estate agents are crucial in the process of buying a home. In the next section we will discuss another alternative, for sale by owners, which has also become popular these days. Even with that model, you still cannot ignore the role of real estate agents.

Real estate agents are professionals. They have in-depth knowledge of the market and properties in the local area. Their negotiation skills can help you get the best outcome from your home purchase. From making an offer to the time your offer is accepted and you complete the purchase involves some form of negotiation. There are a lot of fees involved in buying a house, for which you'll need a real estate agent to help you negotiate and get a better deal than what's on the table. Their negotiation skills usually come from their experience in the industry.

Given their knowledge of the market, they are in the best position to find the right listings that can suit your needs, thanks to the sheer amount of data that these agents have. This also makes them an asset, both for sellers and buyers in the market.

A good real estate agent is one of the most useful resources you can use in the market. They have worked with many experts in the field, including real estate attorneys, title attorneys, home inspectors, and mortgage consultants, all of whom will be useful to you at some point in your purchase journey. Given these connections, it's in your best interest to have a professional real estate agent working with you on your home purchase.

Finally, there are many times when a good deal goes off the rails because either the seller or buyer failed to meet certain deadlines. This creates unnecessary problems, and in many cases, the resolution may be costly. Real estate agents help you by managing the transaction and deadlines so that you can avoid such issues. Beyond the contract, they'll also ensure things like repairs and inspections are correctly completed and on time.

For Sale by Owner (FSBO)

As you search for the right home, you may come across FSBO listings. These are listings where the seller decided to bypass a real estate agent so that they don't have to pay seller's commission on the transaction. What are the ramifications of such an arrangement for you, the buyer?

Well, for starters, the fact that the seller has chosen not to include an agent in their arrangement doesn't mean that you shouldn't. The purchase process is still the same regardless of whether you have an agent or not. This means that you'll still need to determine whether the sale price is fair; get the house inspected; recommend any changes, repairs, or upgrades; make the seller an offer; and when possible, negotiate the best deal.

You must be cautious with FSBO arrangements because, often, sellers price their homes according to their assessment of prices of similar homes in their neighborhood. This may not mean that their prices are fair or reflect the true value of the house.

Some important information you must find out includes whether the property was ever listed by an agent before the seller listed it as FSBO and, if so, for how long. You also need to find out how long the property has been available for sale. If it's been on the market too long, and no one is making offers, there may be something questionable about the property.

FSBO arrangements doesn't mean that you won't need an agent or any of the other professionals relevant to the transaction. For example, in the previous section, we discussed the importance of real estate agents. With this in mind, and considering the possible caveats of FSBO listings, do you think it would be wise to take the seller's word without consulting with an expert? Probably not.

Apart from that, you'll also need to contact the relevant attorneys according to the requirements of your state. In some jurisdictions, both the seller and buyer must have an attorney present. In some states you can do without an attorney, as the closing agreements can be handled by lenders or the company issuing the title. Whichever the case, it's always best to use all the experts available to you, where necessary, to scrutinize the contract and make sure you are not buying your way into a world of trouble.

The other contentious issue will be how to handle the escrow when you decide to buy the house. Certainly, this cannot be done by the seller. The best solution is to have a listing agent hold the money in good faith until you are ready to close on the house. If neither of you involve a real estate agent, you can still have a title company or an attorney act as the intermediary and hold the funds in an escrow.

Finally, even if you have an honest seller or someone you know personally, you should never ignore home inspection services. It doesn't matter whether you are buying the house from your cousin or friend. You must still know the true condition of the house you are buying. You may not be the final occupant of that house, so, to avoid unsightly surprises in the future, it's good to hire a home inspector to check and ensure everything in the house is up to standard.

A FSBO listing may seem like a good idea for savings on commissions and other costs for the seller, however the absence of a real estate agent, on their end, means that you and your team of professionals will have to do most of the leg work to determine the true value of the house and obtain the best deal.

Choosing an Ideal Neighborhood

Are you buying a house in the right neighborhood? Finding the perfect house that meets all your needs may not be the dream you've imagined all along. Everything you've always wanted can turn into a nightmare simply because you bought the perfect house in the wrong neighborhood. You'd be surprised at the number of times homeowners have been in this predicament. Your only option may be to sell the house and move to a different, more welcoming neighborhood or to brave the discomfort and live in your house.

As you are looking for the perfect house, it's equally important to make sure it's in the right neighborhood. The right neighborhood is about more than having neighbors you can relate to. It's about looking at factors that will influence your life and support your overall happiness in that house. Let's look at some important factors that can help you identify the right location below:

1. The Right Budget

In Part 1 of this book, we discussed some important points to answer the question: *How much house can you afford?* This discussion wasn't futile. A good house in the right neighborhood must fit your budget. Otherwise, the cost of keeping the house may have a negative impact on your finances.

You may find similar homes with different prices in different areas. Are you willing to pay a higher price to live in a certain neighborhood, or would it be okay to take the same house, but for a lower price, in another neighborhood? This is a subjective question. Your answers will depend on factors unique to you. So, think about it and consider the features of the house that are important to you.

What are your financial goals and plans? How does the house fit into those plans? A common decision many people make is between paying too much to live in the city or living in the suburbs at a fraction of what it costs to live in the city. Owing to their unique dynamics, some neighborhoods and even cities are more affordable to live in than others. Remember that affordability may also come at a cost. If so, what are you willing to give up to enjoy the lower costs?

2. Lifestyle and Convenience

A house that stifles your lifestyle will not work for you in the long run. There's a certain way that you and your household like to do things. This is who you are. Now imagine buying a house that forces you to change. This is where lifestyle and convenience come in when choosing a neighborhood.

This is a decision that must be made after considering many other factors. Perhaps it's easier for you to switch from a 20-minute commute to work to a 40-minute commute, however, your family may not have the same sentiments. Choose a neighborhood that doesn't necessarily affect your personal life in that manner.

What are some of the things that you are currently used to? Imagine the restaurants, hospitals, parks, and other outdoor facilities. The challenge many people have is that they find it difficult to admit whether or how such things are important in their lives. There's nothing to be ashamed of. Some of these are purely convenience choices, but they have made life easier for you for many years. When choosing a neighborhood, you should think about access to such points too, or you'll be living in a beautiful house that results in boredom in your life.

3.   Future Growth Plans

Before choosing a neighborhood, ask yourself what your future plans are and whether you see them aligning with that neighborhood. Where do you see yourself in 5, 10, or 20 years from now? How long do you think you'll stay in this neighborhood?

Think wholesome. Don't restrict yourself to the basics, like schools for your kids. You should also think of things that may be considered unusual, such as easy access to customers, in case you intend to start a business. Perhaps you are young and attracted to the exciting nightlife in that neighborhood. Will this still be the case in ten years?

Ultimately, the right decision should be a home that checks as many boxes in your life as possible. Some of the factors may be unconventional to many people, however, what matters is that they make sense to you. After all, you are not buying a house for the rest of society, right?

4. Social Factors

There are many social factors that you'll need to look at when choosing a house. Start with the transportation system. For drivers, think about the cost of transportation in terms of how much more or less you'll need to spend on gas to get to work, drive the kids to school, and so on. Don't ignore anything here, as prices fluctuate frequently. If you use public transportation, how easy is it to access the main modes of transport? How far is it from your house? Is it safe? What are some of the issues people have had with public transportation in the recent past?

Where will your kids go to school? Are you happy with the available options? Will your kids fit in seamlessly? Do your kids have to change schools? What if they have difficulties settling in? Are there other alternatives? Maybe your kids are in elementary school right now. Would they feel at home in the middle and high schools within that neighborhood?

Review the local crime statistics to determine whether it's a safe place to live or not. Compare the crime rate with your previous residence. Compare the crime rates for different parts of that state to see whether you are moving to a better or worse place.

5. Associations

Neighborhood associations wield more power than you may imagine. How active is the association where you currently live? How does this compare with the new neighborhood? Some associations are strict on things like the appearance of your home, such that they have certain standards for maintenance that must be adhered to by everyone in the neighborhood. This may mean increased repair and maintenance costs that you may not have planned for. Can you adjust for that? Remember that every homeowners' association is unique in its mandates and how they exercise their duties. Before you choose a neighborhood, learn about their associations, the cost of membership, and the terms of membership.

Once you've determined all the necessary information about the neighborhood and are certain you've settled on the best option, you can now look at the unique features of the house. Start with the size. Is it acceptable for you? Will it still be sufficient in 20 years, or will the space be too large for you? Do you intend to live in this home forever, or are you planning to sell the house some years down the line?

If you are a hands-on kind of person, you may love the idea of having a yard to yourself. There's so much you can do with yard space. You may think of all the projects you can create, how you'll cultivate your hobbies, and potentially create and grow a business out of it. Are you a concrete person who dislikes green landscape? It's nothing to be ashamed of. Some people don't feel comfortable around nature for different reasons. While the presence of trees in the neighborhood may create a calming feeling for some people, it may make you feel uneasy.

Everything we've discussed in this chapter eventually comes down to personal preferences. What works for you may not work for someone else, and that's okay. Remember that buying a house is a huge financial commitment, one that can make your life unnecessarily miserable if you don't choose wisely.

Chapter 10:

Securing a Down Payment

One of the first things to think of when planning to obtain a mortgage for a house is the amount of down payment you need to put down on the house. The market allows a lot of flexibility on this, which also creates room for ambiguities. From time to time, you may hear people suggest a certain percentage for different reasons. Some suggest it's better to pay more. Why?

Let's start with the basics. A down payment is the portion of the home purchase that will not be financed through a mortgage. It is the part of your purchase that you must pay upfront, usually the first solid sign of your commitment to the purchase. In terms of ownership, it's safe to say the down payment is your equity in the property. The terms of your down payment will depend on the type of mortgage you take.

Here's a simple example to explain how down payments work:

Let's say you are buying a house worth $300,000, and you are willing to put down a 10% down payment on the house ($30,000). You'll take out a mortgage worth $270,000, not for the full amount of $300,000. In lending terms, this is called the loan to value ratio (LTV). In the example above, a down payment of 10% means your LTV is 90%. The LTV is also what lenders use to explain the maximum amount they can issue as a loan on the property.

In our opening paragraph, we mentioned that some people suggest it's wise to pay more. In general practice, this is true. A higher down payment signifies a larger commitment on your part. This is encouraging for the lender, and it may even make it easier for you to get approved. In some cases, you can use a larger down payment to negotiate a lower interest rate than what you were initially offered.

Another reason why it's good to consider a larger down payment is to improve your bargaining position in terms of your credit rating. It's common knowledge that a low credit rating may make it difficult, or even impossible, to get any form of financing. The few lenders who may extend you an offer will charge relatively higher interest rates on the loan product. Putting a larger down payment increases your chances of getting a better deal.

One of the subjects we discussed in Chapter 5, as one of the closing costs, was mortgage insurance. Many first-time homebuyers have difficulty raising the down payment. The down payment is one of the main reasons why many people think they cannot afford to buy a house. One way around this is to look for loans that accept lower down payments. Unfortunately, most of these products insist that lenders must buy mortgage insurance.

Mortgage insurance is simply the lender's way of protecting their interests in the contract in the unlikely event that you are unable to honor your obligation in the contract. Terms of mortgage insurance vary from one lender to the next, but on average most lenders will demand insurance if you are offering less than 20% of the purchase price as a down payment.

One way to look at mortgage insurance, if it is ever required of you, is that it is something that gives you a boost in your pursuit of a home. Using our earlier example, a 20% down payment on a $300,000 house is $60,000. How long would it take you to raise this much money? How much must you save every month? Because of such complexities it makes sense to find a solution that can give your homeownership plans a boost.

Minimum Down Payment Requirements

Let's start by debunking a common myth about down payments. There's no set limit that applies to all mortgage plans. The expected minimum depends on the type of home you are buying, the market price of the house, and most importantly, the type of mortgage plan you are going for. While some lenders may ask for a 20% down payment, some may ask for 0%.

Most people worry about 20% while there are properties where lenders may ask for more. The lesson here is that a down payment percentage is not cast in stone. Whichever the case, you can always negotiate the terms of the mortgage and potentially pay less. The minimum down payment requirement should not limit you. If you feel you can deposit more and it suits your plans, go ahead. This will reduce your mortgage liability each month, freeing up your money for other commitments.

Following the subprime mortgage crisis of 2008, otherwise known as the global financial crisis (2007-2010), the US government took over privately held mortgage companies Fannie Mae and Freddie Mac to restore order in the housing market. With government backing, these mortgage companies offer stability and liquidity in the market, which resulted in mortgages becoming more affordable. This is in line with the government's plan to open the housing market and make it easier for more people to become homeowners.

Because of this backing you can now access mortgages with down payments lower than 20%. However, there's still a risk that many borrowers may be unable to keep up the mortgage payments, even with the low down payments. Therefore, you may be asked to buy mortgage insurance, as we explained earlier in this chapter.

Today, the mortgage market is so open that you can secure a mortgage of up to 97% of the price of the house. Yes, you can buy a house with a 3% down payment! Government-backed mortgages like USDA, FHA, and VA generally require the lowest down payments from borrowers. This still depends on other factors like your credit score. You can even get a mortgage with a 0% down payment on these plans.

If you are applying for a jumbo loan, you may need a down payment of 10%. Many first-time homebuyers generally don't apply for these products. The required down payment for jumbo loans can even be larger than 20%, depending on the type and value of the house you wish to buy along with your credit rating.

The 20% Misconception

From our discussions so far, most of what you've probably heard about a 20% down payment is a misconception. We've already seen that you can secure a mortgage with a 3% down payment. If this is the case, then why do people hold onto this notion of 20%?

Well, this idea comes from the fact that most mortgages require a down payment of 20%, or you'll need to pay for mortgage insurance. Depending on how you look at it, a 20% down payment isn't exactly a bad idea either. Your pending balance will be lower, which is a good thing, as you'll pay off the mortgage faster.

So, you shouldn't buy into the misconception that a 20% down payment is mandatory. It may be in some cases, but not all. Thus, it's fair to say this is not an industry standard requirement.

Between 2019 and 2021 the National Association of Realtors (NAR) suggested that the average median down payment for first-time buyers was only 6%. This is proof that many first-time homebuyers were applying for loan options that accepted considerably lower down payments than 20%.

With this information you can confidently search the market for a house within your budget range and start saving for the down payment. For more information on how to raise money for your down payment, refer to Chapter 3, where we discussed several relatable options.

Whether you choose to secure a 20% down payment or not, you should never lose sight of the big picture. Don't stress yourself with trying to raise a larger down payment at the expense of your emergency savings plan. You have many years to pay off the mortgage, so don't leave yourself too exposed.

Another important point many first-time buyers don't realize is the challenge of raising a larger down payment while simultaneously servicing recurring high-interest debt. Credit cards are the most common form of high-interest debt that many people have. Instead of attempting to raise a larger down payment, focus on reducing high-interest debts. This makes you a more attractive borrower as lenders will see that you are not too leveraged. As a result, you may automatically qualify for lower interest rates on your mortgage, so you may not need the high down payment in the first place.

As you save for a larger down payment, you may also become a victim of time. The real estate sector is one where property prices typically appreciate yearly. Though this is not guaranteed, it is a real possibility. This means that the longer you wait to keep saving for a larger down payment, the greater the risk that you'll buy your desired home at a higher price. Instead of waiting too long, visit your lender and discuss your options. Lock in the price and start your mortgage payments right away.

Are Down Payments Necessary?

Ever wondered why lenders always insist on down payments where applicable? Indeed, there are some mortgage programs that can finance 100% of your home purchase without a down payment, however, most first-time homebuyers cannot meet the qualification terms of such programs.

Lenders insist on a down payment, primarily for security purposes, to protect their interest in the property. This also proves your ability to honor the contract terms. The down payment isn't apart of the mortgage. It is your money, your commitment to paying the mortgage on time. Since your money is on the line, it is believed that you are less likely to default on the mortgage. This is one reason why lenders insist on down payments.

Let's look at another scenario where you are unable to pay the mortgage, and the lender must foreclose your house. If this happens, there's a possibility that the house may sell for a lower amount than your outstanding balance on the mortgage. Assuming you put a down payment of 20%, the lender's exposure will only be 80%. So, if they need to foreclose, they won't have difficulty securing the full amount owed.

Your down payment doesn't solely benefit the lender. You also have some gains in it. For example, think of all the budgeting and discipline that went into raising the down payment. It changes your perspective and approach to personal finances. Once you realize how far you can go, if you are committed, there's so much you can do beyond buying the house. It changes your saving habits and, in most cases, your pursuit of additional income streams.

Ultimately, a down payment is the first true sign that you are ready to own a house. If you look at all the financial sacrifices you made to raise that money, you'll realize that you've come a long way. It prepares you for all the other financial commitments that come once you own the house, including property taxes, repair and maintenance, utility bills, and homeowners' association fees.

We also mentioned the relationship between a 20% down payment and private mortgage insurance. You can talk to your lender and request that they remove the mortgage insurance as long as you've attained 20% equity in the house you buy. How is that so?

Well, your equity in the house represents the value of your ownership in that house. Until you pay off the mortgage, you technically don't own the house. It belongs to the lender. So, you can think of equity as your stake in the house that grows with every mortgage payment you make.

As you make your mortgage payments each month, you should keep a close eye on the value of your house. Your equity increases when the value of the house appreciates. It's like buying stock in a listed company.

Another method of increasing your equity is to pay off the mortgage principal through the mortgage payments you remit each month. Many lenders cancel the private mortgage insurance as soon as you've gained 22% equity in the property. However, you can still talk to them about it once you attain 20%.

With a sizable down payment, you can also become more attractive to sellers and real estate agents. Their interpretation of your down payment is your commitment to buying a house, so they may consider you a more serious buyer than others, giving you a competitive advantage. For example, you may not be the only potential buyer interested in a particular house. The seller might have a few interested parties already. When the seller realizes that you are ready to purchase the home with a sizable down payment, it may be easier for the seller to accept your offer over the others. This is because all interested parties believe that you'll have an easier time securing a mortgage.

You must also be careful not to be subtly coerced into buying a house. Realizing your willingness to commit, some sellers may try to convince you to buy a home that you shouldn't purchase in the first place.

While a down payment is mostly a good idea, you must also be alert to the possible challenges you may experience. First, if you decide to back out of the deal, getting your money back may not be the easiest thing to do. This is possible if you run into some problems and need the money. If you don't have an emergency savings fund, don't commit a large amount to your down payment. It's better to put down a lower amount and keep the rest for emergencies.

Is it possible to get a house without a down payment?

For all that's been said about down payments, it's possible to buy a house without one. This is possible, but only with government-backed mortgages that we discussed throughout this book. It's not possible with conventional loans. If you meet the required criteria, you can apply for a USDA or VA mortgage with no down payment.

When it comes to placing a down payment on a house, almost anything you can think of is possible. The requirements aside, it is a good practice to put down a down payment. It gives you a more realistic outlook of the challenge ahead. If you have difficulties raising the down payment, you may have difficulties meeting the required costs of homeownership. Thus, you may need to take a step back and rethink your plan to buy a house. Maybe you should revise your budget or think of a different neighborhood.

Another good thing about a down payment is that the amount you put forward affects the amount you'll pay every month in mortgage payments. Luckily, there are many calculators online that can simulate your expected payments once you enter the required amounts.

A 20% down payment isn't mandatory. Don't strain yourself unnecessarily to raise that amount. More often, 3% might be all you need.

Chapter 11:

You Need a Backup Plan

Homeownership is awesome. For many people, it is the culmination of years of hard work, sacrifices, and persistent toil. It is a dream coming true. Finally being able to have a house you call your own, no one to bother you with rent or monthly mortgage payments. Owning a home feels so good, as good as achieving financial independence.

In unfortunate circumstances, however, this dream can turn into a nightmare. Things may not always go according to plan. Even the most solid homeownership plan can be undone by factors you may not be able to control. The COVID-19 pandemic caused a lot of job losses that led to foreclosures. The worst that could happen is you'll lose your home and potentially everything you've already invested in it. Yikes! Maybe those renters were right after all!

The reality of life is that unless you are dealing with unscrupulous lenders who are out to bleed you dry, legitimate lenders always have a way out for you. It may cost you a bit, but it's better than losing everything.

Remember that concern and stress when you fall behind on your rent? It gets worse when you are paying a mortgage. You see, the worst that could happen when you fall back on your rent is your landlord evicting you. On the other hand, if you fall back on mortgage payments, you have so much more at stake.

There's the potential damage it could cause to your credit score. A negative report on a defaulted mortgage may be bigger than a report on defaulted rent payments. Unless you act fast and settle with your lender, you could lose your home.

The point of this chapter isn't to scare you or get you worried, but to remind you of the realities of life, and more importantly, help you understand that you have options. You don't have to lose your home. People fall on bad times all the time, but with the right arrangements, they keep their homes. When it comes to homeownership, it's always good to prepare for the worst but hope for the best. That applies to life in general.

If you are making mortgage payments, one thing you must do is be proactive with your money. No one understands your financial situation better than you do. This means that you know ahead of time if the next few weeks or months will be difficult. You know whether you'll meet your mortgage obligations or not. Don't wait until you default. As soon as you see the signs, take action. This will help alleviate unnecessary stress and frustration.

Get in touch with your lender as soon as you notice you'll have problems making your payments. If possible, do so before you miss a payment. Even if things get out of hand and you miss a payment you didn't expect to miss, get in touch with them and have a candid conversation. Most lenders will listen and can help you restructure a new payment plan so you don't lose your home.

Why is it important to contact them before you miss a payment?

As soon as you miss a payment, your lender has the authority to report a delinquency (late payment) on your credit report. This doesn't necessarily mean that they are coming after your house right away. However, be mindful that such a note stays on your credit report for seven years. Imagine how this will affect your ability to enjoy certain services.

There's another possibility that you may not be able to pay your mortgage at all. This is probably the worst possible scenario, but it still doesn't mean that you should lose the house. Let's look at some of the options available to you. Note that the most important thing is to get in touch with your lender or agency as soon as you realize you are in trouble and try to work out a solution.

Forbearance

What's the nature of your financial situation? If it is a temporary setback, your lender can potentially allow you a temporary reprieve so you can either pause your mortgage payments or pay lower amounts until your situation improves. Once you get back on your feet, you can pay back the concessions.

Refinancing Your Loan

If you have a good credit rating but are struggling to pay the mortgage, you may consider refinancing the loan. This is a situation where your lender allows you to pay the mortgage at a lower interest rate, which effectively reduces your monthly payments.

One interesting thing about refinancing the mortgage is that, as it frees up cash for you, you may be able to borrow money from your equity in the house if you need it for an emergency.

Loan Modification

A loan modification program is another way of reducing the amount you pay monthly. There are different types of modification arrangements, so discuss them with your lender to find out what they can offer you. You must also understand the impact of a loan modification arrangement on your credit history. Some lenders pass off debt settlement arrangements as loan modification programs, so you must ensure that you know what you are signing up for.

Debt Settlement

A debt settlement is an arrangement where your lender agrees to accept a lower amount than what you owe on the mortgage. It is also known as debt relief or debt adjustment. Essentially, you pay back the agreed amount in a lump sum. It may be a good arrangement for you in case your financial challenges are permanent and there's no possible way for you to continue making payments. Be mindful that settling the debt for a lower amount means that it will have a negative effect on your credit score.

Repayment Plans

If you have had difficulties with mortgage payments for a while and fallen behind, your lender may allow a repayment plan so that you can get your payments back on track.

These are all good options if you can still afford to live in the house and pay the mortgage under the revised terms. However, you may be in a situation where it's financially impossible to make the mortgage payments and pay the monthly bills. In this case, you'll have to consider the following alternatives:

One, perhaps it's time to sell that house altogether. Selling the house isn't how you imagined things would end, but it may be your best solution to avoid foreclosure and still have some money to keep you going. If you've paid the mortgage for a while and the house is now worth a lot more than what you owe your lender, selling might be a good financial option.

Two, you can rent your house. Think about the neighborhood, the rental prices in similar houses, and do the math. If you can collect a good amount to cover the mortgage payments, put it up for rent. It gets even better if you can fetch more than the mortgage payments. This way, you can pay more toward clearing the debt faster. As you consider this option, remember that as the landlord, you'll still be responsible for taxes, insurance, repairs, and any maintenance costs.

Three, you may consider a short sale. This is ideal in case your outstanding loan amount is larger than the value of the house. In this case, you'll try to convince the lender to accept the price at which the house will sell as full payment for the debt you owe, especially if you end up selling the house at a lower amount. This arrangement is like a debt settlement and will negatively affect your credit score.

Finally, you may also consider a deed in lieu of foreclosure. This is an arrangement where your lender releases you from the mortgage. In exchange, you sign over the deed to the house. It will also leave a negative impact on your credit score.

The most important thing about all the arrangements we've discussed is to understand how they may help you and the impact, if any, that they will have on your credit report. A financial counselor can advise you accordingly on this.

Engaging Your Options

If you are worried about a lender foreclosing on your house because you can't pay your mortgage loan, your concerns are valid. You should consult with a housing counselor approved by the United States Department of Housing and Urban Development (HUD) to assist you on how to avoid a foreclosure.

Your lender will want to know why you feel that you won't be able to make the payments and whether it's a temporary or permanent setback. Remember, that as you speak to them to find a solution, they must also make sure that the solution is in their best interests. If your situation is permanent, it will be difficult to secure an option that won't cost you the house.

For a temporary setback, lenders may be lenient as they consider solutions that may work for both parties. They'll need to know more about your source of income, regular expenses, and if you have other assets. Cash in your bank account will also count as an asset in this case.

A foreclosure is a painful experience for homeowners, and many lenders have programs that can avoid it altogether. When you talk to your lender about this matter, do not leave any stone unturned. Do not misrepresent your financial situation either. Give them the true picture of your reality so that they can find solutions that are tailor-made for you. Otherwise, you may walk away with a solution that will only leave you in more trouble a few months down the line, and they'll have no alternative but to foreclose on the house.

You may be required to apply for a mortgage assistance program. Once your application is reviewed, you'll be advised on the loss mitigation options that apply in your situation, if possible.

The role of a HUD-approved housing counselor is to help you determine your options after understanding your position and recommend additional help or programs that can help you. They will also help you understand your lender's position and the options available to them. They are like a mediator who understands the needs of both parties, only that they are more educational to you than to your lender. Remember that, ultimately, your lender is within their legal right to foreclose on your house if you cannot make the payments by virtue of the contract you signed with them.

The counselor will also take you through the process of negotiating with your lender, essentially preparing you for what lies ahead. They'll also help you with any documents that may be required.

When you get to this point, there's a good chance that you may have other financial challenges, such as credit card debt. Counselors will also help you sort out your finances and give you tips on how to budget properly as you salvage the situation. Some offer this service at a fee, while others do it for free. The goal is to improve your financial well-being.

What if you have already been served with legal papers, and the foreclosure is imminent? Well, it's not all over yet. You can still buy yourself time by consulting with an attorney.

This may be one of the lowest moments in your life, and you are vulnerable. Be careful not to fall for scams. There are many foreclosure scammers who prey on vulnerable homeowners under the guise of helping you avoid the inevitable. Instead, they are only interested in your money. So how do you avoid jumping from the frying pan into the fire? Here are some red flags you should be on the lookout for:

- They promise that they can have your mortgage terms changed. This isn't possible. Your mortgage agreement is a binding contract. The fact that you are unable to pay means you are in breach of that contract. The contract cannot be changed when you are already in breach of it.

- They claim that they work with or are affiliated with the government. They may even have a logo that looks like a government agency's logo but with a slight modification.

- They ask you for payment up front.

- They claim that they will conduct a forensic audit of your mortgage.

- They guarantee that you won't lose your home but don't explain how. The only way your foreclosure can be halted is through a court order. Otherwise, your lender is legally obliged to do what's in their best interest, as per the contract you signed with them.

- They give you documents to sign, which you don't understand, and pressure you into signing them immediately. Never sign anything without consulting your attorney first. Some scammers may ask you to sign over the title of your house to them.

- They recommend that you stop paying your monthly mortgage payments while they sort out your issue.

- They ask you to send payments to another company or person instead of your mortgage lender.

Many people have fallen for such scams in the past, mostly because they were desperate and were afraid of losing their homes. Anyone can fall victim to such scammers. Remember, when your home is on the line, you may not be the best judge of character. You have legal options that can help you save your home from foreclosure. Talk to a HUD-approved housing counselor, and more importantly, engage your lender before things get out of hand.

Staying on Track

Given the dire consequences of falling behind on your mortgage payments, what can you do to ensure that you don't become a victim?

First, remember that if you are still paying for the mortgage, the house belongs to your lender until you complete your last mortgage payment. Since you will be making payments every month until the contract expires, try to find other sources of income. Relying on only one source of income can leave you in a pickle when things are not working out for you at work. A side hustle or a second job may come in handy. Depending on your situation, you may consider having a roommate, or if the house is big enough, an Airbnb business to supplement your mortgage payments.

Buying a house is a huge financial commitment. Before you jump into it, make sure that you are financially prepared for what lies ahead. Learn your credit score and the amount of house you can get with it. Plan for the down payment so that you don't get any surprises along the way. Remember that a down payment is not apart of the mortgage, and it gives you part-ownership of the house from the day you move in.

Assess your financial situation to understand the kind of debts that you owe and work on them. Start by paying off the expensive debts first, like credit cards, so that you can reduce the burden on your money and make it easier to handle mortgage payments. Ultimately, buying a house is like buying a car. It will need repair and maintenance from time to time to ensure that it is in the best condition. Plan for a house with running costs that you can afford, including the cost of utilities and homeowners' association (HOA) fees.

Do not stretch yourself too thin to live in a house. If you can't afford it, there will always be other amazing homes in the market that fall within your budget range. If you push yourself too far, the slightest change in your income will make it harder to keep up with the mortgage payments and maintain your emergency savings fund.

Conclusion

If you've ever bought a used car before, you probably understand some or most of the concerns that go into buying a house. You must ask a lot of questions to ensure that the car will do more than just fit your budget. It can be a useful and reliable tool. Without careful analysis, a used car could turn into a money pit. The same applies when buying a house. There are many things you need to look at, and that's on two fronts—the house and your money.

The core of this book talks about how to save money and buy yourself that house you've been dreaming about. Everything about the house comes down to your money. Can you afford to live in that neighborhood? Will your kids be okay with it? What about the size of the house, the facilities and equipment that comes with it, neighborhood association fees, etc.? All these things cost money. When you start thinking of buying a house, money will always be an important consideration.

Here's the shocker—the financial demands don't end when you buy the house or when you pay your last mortgage installment. As a homeowner, you now assume the status of your landlords from previous tenancy experience. Everything that goes into making sure that the house is in a good livable condition rests on your shoulders. If the kids break anything, you must dig into your pocket and fix it. If the house needs repair work, you're responsible. If the house needs repainting to give it a new look, that's also your responsibility. You can no longer depend on your landlord or management to take care of such things. So, as amazing as it is to finally own your house, you must also understand the long-term financial commitment that comes with owning one. Therefore, we say that owning a house is like buying a used car. If you are not careful with your finances, it could devastate you.

Putting these concerns aside, you don't need to worry about most of these things, and for a good reason. Take a moment and think about how far you have come, from renting a house to finally owning one. There was a time when you probably thought you'd never be able to afford a house. And then you started saving, making changes, budgeting, and planning. Before long, you had a down payment ready. The next thing you knew, you were moving into your house and making mortgage payments. That is real progress.

At times you must push your limits and exit your comfort zone to realize your potential. There's an element of financial discipline that comes with homeownership. It turns you from a spendthrift into someone who's prudent with their money. Perhaps it's the fear of losing your home if you can't make the payments on time that forces you to rethink your perspective and approach to finances. Or maybe it's the realization that you've been hemorrhaging money and you need to plug the leaks. Whichever of these applies to you, the growth that comes with becoming a homeowner is amazing. If you go about it right, you won't have to worry about some of the financial commitments that come with owning a house.

By the time you own a house, you will have picked up some important lessons along the way, especially on saving money. You will have learned how to budget, how to set your financial priorities in order, and, more importantly, how to save. You may have also succeeded in negotiating for better pay, gotten a new job, added a side hustle, or another method of creating additional income streams. These things don't go away because you've finally bought the house. Everyone could use extra money from time to time, even those who seem to have all the money in the world.

The culture of saving doesn't end. Keep it up and use the extra money to cultivate growth in other spheres of your life. Now that you have a house, you could save up and buy a new car, shore up your emergency savings account, save more money for your kids' college needs, or even go for those vacations you denied yourself while saving for your house.

Owning a home is one of the most fulfilling experiences you'll ever have in life. For some, it's the ultimate accomplishment in life, having a place that you can call your own. To achieve this, you must also make sure that everything that went into getting that house was done the right way.

The importance of working with professionals cannot be stressed enough. Do not take anything for granted when it comes to buying a house. Have a professional guiding you at every step of the way. This is particularly important when you are buying a house directly from the seller, without involving any agents. You may be saving a lot on commissions, but unless you are an expert in the field, an expert will help you discover things out about the house that you may not have been able to learn on your own.

As a rule of thumb, don't fall in love with any house. This has led many people to make mistakes and ignore some major red flags. You must be objective regarding everything about the house, which is why you need professionals. Have an inspection done. Even if the seller hires someone for that, spend the extra cash and tag along with your own inspector. Remember that in such situations, everyone always has their own best interests at heart. The seller wants to get rid of their house. Ever wondered why? Why would they want to sell this house that you can't seem to get enough of? That's where your experts come in. They help you see the house beyond its aesthetics. They determine the problems that your seller may not tell you about. They alert you on things that you can overlook and those you can't. From their assessment, you can discuss a potential lower purchase price with the owner.

Finally, take your time. Don't be pressured into buying any house. Remember that whatever house you choose, it should work for you. It should suit your needs, be a comfortable place for your family, and a place where you can enjoy many years of peace. The perfect house may not check all your boxes, but it should check most of them. Now that you are ready to save and own that house, we wish you the best of luck and hope you find a house that becomes your home.

Visit bluepeakpublishing.com to subscribe to our newsletter for fun tips, recipes, giveaways, and information on our latest releases. Also, write us at bookhound@bluepeakpublishing.com for your comments.

References

Araj, V. (2021, December 6). Mortgage Refinancing: What Is It And How Does It Work? Rocketmortgage.com; Rocket Mortgage. https://www.rocketmortgage.com/learn/how-does-refinancing-work

Benefits.gov. (2022). Welcome to Benefits.gov | Benefits.gov. Benefits.gov. https://www.benefits.gov/benefit/401

Braverman, B. (2021, February 8). How does rent-to-own work? Bankrate; Bankrate.com. https://www.bankrate.com/real-estate/how-rent-to-own-works/

Bundrick, H. M. (2018, May 7). What Down Payment Is Required? NerdWallet. https://www.nerdwallet.com/article/mortgages/payment-buy-home

Bundrick, H. M. (2020a, June 12). Government Home Loans: A Comprehensive Guide. NerdWallet. https://www.nerdwallet.com/article/mortgages/government-home-loans

Bundrick, H. M. (2020b, June 30). What Is a USDA Loan? Am I Eligible for One? NerdWallet. https://www.nerdwallet.com/article/mortgages/usda-loan

Coberly, A. (2017, June 12). Pros and Cons of For Sale by Owner: Weighing Your Options. HomeLight Blog; Homelight Inc. https://www.homelight.com/blog/pros-and-cons-of-for-sale-by-owner-weigh-your-options/

Collins, K., & He, R. (2020, June 16). Is Your Credit Score Good Enough to Buy a House? NextAdvisor with TIME.

https://time.com/nextadvisor/mortgages/credit-score-to-buy-a-house/

Consumer Finance Protection Bureau. (2019). CARES Act mortgage forbearance: what you need to know. Consumer Financial Protection Bureau. https://www.consumerfinance.gov/coronavirus/mortgage-and-housing-assistance/cares-act-mortgage-forbearance-what-you-need-know/

Crace, M. (2022, January 20). How Much Do You Need For A Down Payment To Buy A House? Rocketmortgage.com; Rocket Mortgage. https://www.rocketmortgage.com/learn/how-much-down-payment-for-a-house

Fontinelle, A. (2021, September 11). How Much House Can I Afford? Home Affordability Calculator. Forbes. https://www.forbes.com/advisor/mortgages/how-much-house-can-i-afford/

Fontinelle, A., & Cetera, M. (2021, June 9). 10 Tax Benefits Of Owning A Home. Forbes. https://www.forbes.com/advisor/mortgages/tax-benefits-of-owning-a-home/

Hiscock, K. (2017, July 25). What Are The Benefits Of Owning A Home? Https://Www.rochesterrealestateblog.com; Kyle Hiscock. https://www.rochesterrealestateblog.com/benefits-owning-a-home/

Jaffe, J. (2022, January 19). The home office deduction: Why you probably can't claim it, even if you work from home. CNET; CNET. https://www.cnet.com/personal-finance/taxes/home-office-tax-deduction/

Kearns, D. (2022). Understanding Mortgage Closing Costs. Investopedia. https://www.investopedia.com/mortgage/mortgage-guide/closing-costs/

Kearns, D., & Marquand, B. (2019, September 9). Mortgage Closing Costs: How Much You'll Pay. NerdWallet. https://www.nerdwallet.com/article/mortgages/closing-costs-mortgage-fees-explained

Kielar, H. (2022). Government Home Loans And More: A Guide For First-Time Borrowers. Rocketmortgage.com; Rocket Mortgage. https://www.rocketmortgage.com/learn/government-loans#:~:text=Housing%20loans%20are%20not%20directly,the%20Native%20American%20Direct%20Loan.

Lankford, K., & Ortiz, J. (2022). Can You Take the Home Office Deduction? US News & World Report; U.S. News & World Report. https://money.usnews.com/money/personal-finance/taxes/articles/guide-to-home-office-tax-deduction

Lerner, M. (2021, December 9). How to save money on closing costs. Washington Post; The Washington Post. https://www.washingtonpost.com/business/2021/12/01/how-save-money-closing-costs/

Marquand, B. (2016, March 14). Tax Deductions for Homeowners. NerdWallet. https://www.nerdwallet.com/article/mortgages/tax-deductions-for-homeowners

Marquand, B., & Bell, L. (2018, May 7). VA Loans: How They Work, Who Qualifies. NerdWallet. https://www.nerdwallet.com/article/mortgages/va-home-loan

Marquit, M. (2021, June 2). The Tax Benefits of Owning a Home: Must-Know Deductions and Credits. Credible; Credible. https://www.credible.com/blog/mortgages/tax-benefits-owning-home/

McWhinney, J. (2022). How Much Mortgage Can You Afford? Investopedia. https://www.investopedia.com/articles/pf/05/030905.asp

Morris, G. (2021, November 9). Pros & Cons of Home Ownership | Homebuyer Education. InCharge Debt Solutions. https://www.incharge.org/housing/homebuyer-education/homeownership-guide/advantages-and-disadvantages-of-owning-a-home/

O'Shea, B., & Wood, K. (2017, September 19). The Credit Score Needed to Buy a House. NerdWallet. https://www.nerdwallet.com/article/mortgages/whats-exact-credit-score-need-buy-home

Parker, T. (2022). Top Tax Advantages of Buying a Home. Investopedia. https://www.investopedia.com/articles/personal-finance/051915/what-are-tax-advantages-when-buying-home.asp

Porter, T. (2021, October 21). What is home down payment? Bankrate; Bankrate.com. https://www.bankrate.com/mortgages/what-is-down-payment/

Pritchard, J. (2013). What Is Rent-to-Own? The Balance. https://www.thebalance.com/what-is-rent-to-own-315664

Proctor, C. (2021, December 23). What credit score is needed to buy a house? It varies by loan type. Business Insider; Insider. https://www.businessinsider.com/personal-finance/what-credit-score-is-needed-to-buy-a-house?r=US&IR=T

Quicken Loans. (2022). What Credit Score Do You Need To Buy A House In 2022? Quickenloans.com; Quicken Loans. https://www.quickenloans.com/learn/credit-score-to-buy-a-house

Rae, D. (2021, June 28). The Home Office Deduction 2020 In Time Of Coronavirus. Forbes. https://www.forbes.com/sites/davidrae/2020/05/06/home-office-deduction-2020/?sh=72114b307f75

Segal, T. (2022). Federal Housing Administration (FHA) Loan. Investopedia. https://www.investopedia.com/terms/f/fhaloan.asp

Sharkey, S. (2021). 8 Tax Deductions For Homeowners: Your Breaks And Benefits. Rocketmortgage.com; Rocket Mortgage. https://www.rocketmortgage.com/learn/tax-deductions-for-homeowners

Tarpley, L. G. (2021, May 19). 7 tips for choosing a neighborhood when you're ready to buy a home. Business Insider; Insider. https://www.businessinsider.com/personal-finance/how-to-choose-location-buying-home?r=US&IR=T

Uhlig, D. K. (2012). The Importance of Having a Professional Real Estate Agent. Home Guides | SF Gate. https://homeguides.sfgate.com/importance-having-professional-real-estate-agent-49440.html

Weintraub, E. (2021a). 8 Reasons to Buy a Home. The Balance. https://www.thebalance.com/eight-reasons-to-buy-a-home-1798233#:~:text=The%20pride%20of%20ownership%2C%20home,mortgage%20reduction%2C%20and%20equity%20loans.

Weintraub, E. (2021b). For Sale by Owner: What Is Involved In Buying a Home Without a Seller's Agent? The Balance. https://www.thebalance.com/buying-for-sale-by-owner-1798295

Wichter, Z. (2022a). How Much House Can I Afford? | Bankrate | New House Calculator. Bankrate. https://www.bankrate.com/calculators/mortgages/new-house-calculator.aspx

Wichter, Z. (2022b, January 13). Mortgage relief: What to know about mortgage forbearance. Bankrate; Bankrate.com. https://www.bankrate.com/mortgages/everything-you-should-know-about-mortgage-forbearance/

Williams, G. (2021). Renting vs. Buying a Home: Which Is Smarter? US News & World Report; U.S. News & World Report. https://realestate.usnews.com/real-estate/articles/renting-vs-buying-a-home-which-is-smarter

Made in the USA
Monee, IL
07 July 2026